NAVIGATING
the JOURNEY
of a LIFETIME

DONNA P. TURNER

ISBN 978-1-64670-684-6 (Paperback)
ISBN 978-1-64670-685-3 (Hardcover)
ISBN 978-1-64670-686-0 (Digital)

Covenant Books, Inc.
11661 Hwy 707
Murrells Inlet, SC 29576
www.covenantbooks.com

CONTENTS

ACKNOWLEDGEMENTS

T his book is dedicated to my amazing daughter, Genesis. Genesis, you are truly the quintessential of grace, uniqueness, and beauty. Thank you for your words of encouragement, patience, love, humor, and for reminding me of what is most important in life. I love you dearly. Always remember to TRUST YOUR JOURNEY!—Mom

I would be remiss if I did not acknowledge those individuals who have prayed for me and encouraged me throughout my personal journey. I would like to thank my Mom, Dad, Stepmom, Uncle LeRoy and Aunt San, and my brother and sisters, for their constant support, prayers, and words of encouragement—I AM BECAUSE OF YOU!! Special thanks to my amazing pastor and his lovely wife, Steve and Deidre Green, for your prayers and support. Pastor Green, thank you for believing in me and giving me an opportunity to write my first article for The Informer fifteen years ago. I would also like to thank my church family and friends for your prayers, love, and support. Special thanks to Tarsha Bluiett, Joe Clark, Tammy Fincher, Aeyesha Green, Charlotte Jenkins, Carol Johnson, Elatio Johnson, Jameria Johnson, Janice Johnson, Tyrone Jones, Don Scott, Ursula Smith, Shaun Stokes, Sandra Rhodes, Janice Strickland, Pat Talley,

Regina Taylor, Jackie Wells, Torrence White, and Elvira Parks for your invaluable support and input on this project. And last but not least, thank you Holy Spirit for guiding me every step of the way throughout my life's journey—I love you!!!

INTRODUCTION

Space: the final frontier. These are the voyages of the starship Enterprise. Its five-year mission: to explore strange new worlds, to seek out new life and new civilizations, to boldly go where no man has gone before. (Star Trek opening monologue, 1966-1969)

This statement was popularized by the series *Star Trek* in the mid to late 1960s. Although this statement describes a group of individuals on a quest to discover unexplored territory, I believe it has a significant meaning in the life of every believer. Indulge me for a moment as I paint the backdrop for this book. For the crew aboard the starship Enterprise, the final frontier was Space or that last unexplored area not yet discovered by man. The crew knew their mission and the perils associated with such a journey. The last portion of the phrase, "to boldly go where no man has gone before," suggests a courageous embarking into a territory that many simply refused to undertake.

It has been suggested that the *Star Trek* monologue was taken from a White House booklet published in 1958 that was written to garner support for a national space program in the wake of the first artificial earth satellite, Sputnik, being launched into space by the Soviet Union. The passage taken from the booklet reads:

> The first of these factors is the compelling urge of man to explore and to discover, the thrust of curiosity that leads men to try to go where no one has gone before. (The White House, 1958)

The Soviet Union had accomplished at that time what others, including the United States, had only hoped to accomplish first. Now, let me embellish a bit here. Against all odds, the Sputnik was launched and had catapulted the rest of the world into a heightened awareness and more focused push to establish or strengthen its own national space program. For the United States, the National Aeronautics and Space Administration (NASA) was established to replace its predecessor, the National Advisory Committee for Aeronautics (NACA) in 1958, almost one year after the launch of Sputnik. The NASA program was created to oversee the nation's civilian space program and to engage in peaceful space and aeronautics research. NASA is also responsible for ensuring that the twenty-four-satellite system that comprises the Global Positioning System (GPS) is operating efficiently. The United States, who appeared to lag behind in space research and technology, has now become the world's forerunner in these endeavors. Twelve years later, the United States successfully launched its first manned flight to the moon and has since been the forerunner in conducting successful manned flights to the moon.

Anyone embarking on a journey must first consider the cost and if they are willing to endure the uncertainties of such a journey. Consider the life of noted abolitionist, Frederick Douglass. Douglass was born into slavery around 1818 in Talbot County, Maryland. Separated at birth from his mother, he spent the first six years of his life with his grandmother before being sent to Colonel Lloyd's plantation where he had his first encounter with slavery. Under the care of "Aunt Katy," Douglass was often subject to hunger, ridicule, and beatings. He was the "property" of several individuals, each providing experiences that would equip him with the knowledge, fortitude, and passion that he would need throughout his journey as a slave and as a free man. One of his first property owners, Sophia Auld, taught him the alphabet until her husband, Hugh Auld, forbade her. Hugh said that "learning will do him no good, but a great deal of harm, making him disconsolate and unhappy" (Douglass, 1962). This dialogue provided Douglass with a new insight to his then present position. While suggesting that "knowledge unfits a child to be a slave," Douglass realized that knowledge was in fact "the direct pathway from slavery to freedom" (Douglass, 1962).

> "To enslave a man successfully and safely, it is necessary to keep their minds occupied with thoughts and aspirations short of the liberty of which they are deprived (p. 147)."

Douglass was determined to learn how to read and write regardless of the consequences that awaited him if he were discovered. So resolute was he about educating himself with hopes of eventual freedom, that he was placed under the "care" of Edward Covey, a farmer known to break the "will" of slaves.

Under Covey, Douglass experienced numerous beatings for his stubbornness and attempts at escape. Once, he was beaten so badly that he ran to his "property owner" with hopes of finding some sort of reprieve only to be told that he had to return to Covey to fulfil the remainder of his contracted obligations. For his crime, Covey was determined to inflict upon him a beating that would surely result in his death; however, this time he refused him. That day, Douglass made up his mind that he would never be beat again. This was a significant turning point in Douglass's life-he was no longer afraid to die and that in and of itself had made him free.

Frederick Douglass's life seemed dismal and his fate certain. His prevailing thought, "I am a slave for life", was ever before him. He could have given up his hopes of one day being a free man and accepted life as a slave—but he did not. He vowed that he would escape slavery and on September 3, 1838, disguised as a free black sailor and equipped with knowledge and skills that would aid him in his escape, he did. He knew that along this precarious journey he could be betrayed by individuals who might recognize him and could benefit from his capture. He also knew the penalty if captured, but he never looked back. Frederick Douglass went on to become a prolific writer, orator, social reformer, United States Ambassador to Haiti, and advisor to former President Abraham Lincoln. He became a national leader in the abolitionist movement and despite mocking, insult, and violent personal attacks, never waned in his commitment to the cause.

Dr. Martin Luther King Jr. was a social activist who played a key role in the American civil rights movement from the mid-1950s until his assassination in 1968. Inspired by advocates of nonviolence like Mahatma Gandhi, Leo Tolstoy, and Reinhold Niebuhr, Dr. King sought equality for African Americans, the economically disadvantaged and victims of injustice through peaceful protests. He was considered to be the driving force behind watershed events like the Montgomery Bus Boycott of 1955 and the March on Washington in 1963. During his journey as a civil rights activist, Dr. King faced much opposition, suffering, threats, and danger. When Dr. King accepted the call as one of the key leaders and spokesman of the civil rights movement, he knew that he and his family would be in constant danger. He knew the undertakings and perils of this journey, and yet he accepted. On April 12, 1965, Dr. King and several noted civil rights activists led a demonstration to bring national attention to the brutal, racist treatment suffered by blacks in one of the most segregated cities in America—Birmingham, Alabama. For months, an organized boycott of the city's white-owned-and-operated businesses had failed to achieve any substantive results, leaving King and others convinced they had no other options but to ignore a recently passed ordinance that prohibited public gathering without an official permit. Several clergy criticized King for these direct actions calling them untimely and unwarranted. It was this criticism that led King to pen one of his greatest texts on the civil rights movement.

You may well ask: "Why direct action? Why sit ins, marches and so forth? Isn't negotiation a better path?" You are quite right in calling for negotiation. Indeed, this is the very purpose of direct action. Nonviolent direct action seeks to create such a crisis and foster such a tension that a community which has constantly refused to negotiate is forced to confront the issue. It seeks so to dramatize the issue that it can no longer be ignored. My citing the creation of tension as part of the work of the nonviolent resister may sound rather shocking. But I must confess that I am not afraid of the word "tension." I have earnestly opposed violent tension, but there is a type of constructive, nonviolent tension which is necessary for growth. Just as Socrates felt that it was necessary to create a tension in the mind so that individuals could rise from the bondage of myths and half truths to the unfettered realm of creative analysis and objective appraisal, so must we see the need for nonviolent gadflies to create the kind of tension in society that will help men rise from the dark depths of prejudice and racism to the majestic heights of understanding and brotherhood. The purpose of our direct-action program is to create a situation so crisis packed that it will inevitably open the door to negotiation. I therefore concur with you in your call for negotiation. Too long has our beloved Southland been bogged down in a tragic effort to live in monologue rather than dialogue.

We know through painful experience that freedom is never voluntarily given by the oppressor; it must be demanded by the oppressed. Frankly, I have yet to engage in a direct-action campaign that was "well timed" in the view of those who have not suffered unduly from the disease of segregation. For years now, I have heard the word "Wait!" It rings in the ear of every Negro

with piercing familiarity. This "Wait" has almost
always meant "Never." We must come to see,
with one of our distinguished jurists, that "justice
too long delayed is justice denied." (King, 1965)

Some of the fruits of his labor include the enacting of the Civil
Rights Act of 1964 and the Voting Rights Act of 1965. Additionally,
King was awarded the Nobel Peace Prize in 1964. This distinction
was given to those who have done the most or the best work for the
fraternity between nations, for the abolition or reduction of standing armies, and for the holding and promotion of peace congresses.
Dr. King could have chosen another life's journey. He could have
succumbed to his personal fears and insecurities and decided that
the time was not right for such a move. Instead, however, he forged
ahead in the midst of his tears and tumultuous situation in the south
and became one of the most prominent leaders of the civil rights
movement. Yes, he died an untimely death, but his legacy lives on.

In the midst of a male-dominated society, Susan B. Anthony
was an advocate for women's suffrage. She was one of the leading
voices for the rights and equal treatment of women. Anthony advo-
cated for equal treatment and pay for women, the right to purchase
and own land, the formation of Working Women's Association, and
the right for women to vote. Throughout her tenure as a women's
rights advocate, Anthony was ostracized, persecuted, and arrested for
her stance on women's rights.

It was we, the people; not we, the white
male citizens; nor yet we, the male citizens; but
we, the whole people, who formed the Union.

And we formed it, not to give the blessings of liberty, but to secure them; not to the half of ourselves and the half of our posterity, but to the whole people—women as well as men. And it is a downright mockery to talk to women of their enjoyment of the blessings of liberty while they are denied the use of the only means of securing them provided by this democratic-republican government—the ballot.

For any State to make sex a qualification that must ever result in the disfranchisement of one entire half of the people is to pass a bill of attainder, or an ex post facto law, and is therefore a violation of the supreme law of the land. By it the blessings of liberty are forever withheld from women and their female posterity. To them this government has no just powers derived from the consent of the governed. To them this government is not a democracy. It is not a republic. It is an odious aristocracy; a hateful oligarchy of sex; the most hateful aristocracy ever established on the face of the globe; an oligarchy of wealth, where the rich govern the poor. An oligarchy of learning, where the educated govern the ignorant, or even an oligarchy of race, where the Saxon rules the African, might be endured; but this oligarchy of sex, which makes father, brothers, husband, sons, the oligarchs over the mother and sisters, the wife and daughters of every household--which ordains all men sovereigns, all women subjects, carries dissension, discord and rebellion into every home of the nation.

Webster, Worcester and Bouvier all define a citizen to be a person in the United States, entitled to vote and hold office.

The only question left to be settled now is: Are women persons? And I hardly believe any of our opponents will have the hardihood to say they are not. Being persons, then, women are citizens; and no State has a right to make any law, or to enforce any old law, that shall abridge their privileges or immunities. (Anthony, 1873)

Anthony's words still resonate in the hearts of women across the country who are fighting for equality in position and pay. The endeavors of Anthony and other proponents for women's rights resulted in the admission of women in Rochester University for the first time in 1900 and the Susan B. Anthony Amendment allowing women to vote. Anthony knew the undertakings and painstaking consequences of her journey yet decided to embark upon this journey despite what lay ahead.

Isabella Baumfree, an African-American abolitionist and women's rights activist, was born a slave in upstate New York in c. 1797 to slave owners. Convinced that God called her to leave the city to preach the truth of his word throughout the nation, Isabella and her infant child walked to freedom in 1826. As a result, in 1843, Isabella Baumfree changed her name to Sojourner Truth. She traveled throughout the US advocating for the abolition of slavery and voting rights for African-American women. Truth delivered one of the most profound speeches that criticized racial and gender inequalities at the Ohio Women's Rights Convention in Akron Ohio.

> If the first woman God ever made was strong enough to turn the world upside down all alone, these women together ought to be able to turn it back, and get it right side up again! And now they is asking to do it, the men better let them. (Sojourner Truth, 1851)

Truth lived during a time of injustice and oppression where slavery was still the norm and women were considered property. She did not allow the context of the times to thwart that which she believed was a God-given assignment.

The accomplishments of NASA, Frederick Douglass, Dr. King, Susan B. Anthony, and Sojourner Truth are still felt throughout our nation today.

I contemplated a number of different ways to start this book. There were several quotes and scriptures that I could have used, but I decided to start with the *Star Trek* monologue because it captures the heart of what so many have felt at some point in life's journey. This imaginary Enterprise traveled the universe exploring uncharted territory. Its mission was to go where no man or woman had ever gone before. This is what was accomplished through Sputnik and eventually through the endeavors of NASA and by anyone who has taken a journey into unchartered territory. Dr. King, Susan B. Anthony, and Sojourner Truth each embarked on selfless journeys that threatened their lives at every turn, but yet they stayed the course.

All of us are on a journey whether we realize it or not. Throughout our journey, we are bombarded with ideas from our communities, our culture, our institutions of learning, our families, and society that shape our perceptions of who we are and subsequently the world around us. Growing up in the 1970s and 1980s, I was inundated with notions of beauty from society and from my culture. Billboards were saturated with images of women who wore a size 0 or 2 in clothing, donned naturally straight or curly locks, and were a towering 5'6" or taller in height (this gives you an inclination to my petite stature). In my mind, if this indeed was society's only idea of beauty, then I was out on all counts. I began to question God about "natural selection"—why were some individuals graced with what was considered desirable characteristics and others were not? What was more disconcerting than society's idea of beauty was that my own culture had taken on these same notions of beauty. For example, during those days, if you had light complexion and long hair, you were considered pretty. If you were dark skinned with short hair, you were not considered attractive. Well, I was dark skinned with short hair. Again, I felt as though I had struck out in society and within my own culture. I found safety in talking to God because I could not talk to anyone else. Serious conversations were for adults, and children were often told to be quiet and go outside and play. I also found safety in fantasizing about a life where there was no financial struggle and one in which I had long hair and wore the latest `fashion. My sister and I would pretend that we had long hair by placing towels on our heads and modeling our beauty by walking down our imaginary runway. I was often reminded of my "undesirable traits" from those with a "desirable traits."

I remember telling some of my classmates of my intention to become a member of a prestigious sorority when I enrolled in college. One young lady said that you have to be light skinned in order to become a member of that sorority. Although that was not the case, that statement further deepened the negative view that I had of myself. That statement and more like it in later years deepened my need for affirmation. Although society is more gracious and more accepting of cultural diversity, I find that the former notions of beauty still hover over the minds of this generation.

I recently spoke at a girls' empowerment seminar. I was one of several speakers. My topic was image. I did a modified version of Dr. Kenneth Clark's doll experiment. In Dr. Clark's 1940s experiment, he placed a black doll and a white doll before some African-American children. He posed the following question: (1) Which doll is the pretty doll? (2) Which doll is the nice doll? (3) Which doll is the bad doll? The children responded that the white doll was the pretty doll, the white doll was the nice doll, and the black doll was the bad doll, respectively. I placed two African-American dolls before girls ranging in age from twelve through seventeen. One doll was very dark skinned with very short hair, and the other doll was light in complexion with long flowing hair. I asked the girls to rate the dolls on beauty using a scale of one to ten with ten being the highest. The darker Barbie doll's scores ranged from two through eight while the lighter Barbie doll received an overwhelming vote of ten. I am simply trying to demonstrate this one example of how prejudice within cultures can affect one's perception of image. This is just one example in the minutiae of life.

Again, some of the data that we receive is valuable, and some is not. Some of this data may or may not bias our thinking regarding ourselves, our relationships, and our worldview. At the beginning of our journey, many of us were passively engaged in our journey as life was "happening" to us. We were passive receivers of this influx of "stuff." We did not or could not process or reflect on what was happening to us.

Growing up, I was told that you had to go to school to "make" something of yourself and upon graduation a choice had to be made. In some cultures, it is understood that men work and support their families and women stay home and care for the children and took care of the affairs of the home. Whatever the scenario, a choice had to be made. As I stated earlier, I often talked to God about my station in life. I read the big white Bible that was on our living room table with hope of gaining an understanding about life. While I never gained a good understanding about why things were the way they were for me at that age, I found myself being drawn into a relationship with God. At the age of twelve, I gave my life to Christ. When I graduated from high school, I went to college, graduated, went to graduate school, and got a good job without good pay, got married, had beautiful little girl, and began to age gracefully. I quit my job, got a divorce, and I thought I was going to lose my mind. All of this sent me reeling. My life was in total chaos, utter disarray. There was no more normalcy, at least not as the world would define it. I found myself in unfamiliar territory, which drove me crazy, especially for someone like me who thrives on stability and normalcy. I didn't take chances and definitely did not live my life on the edge. I don't even like heights much less edges or ledges. But to attain greatness requires a sacrifice.

Jeanne Guyon, a French mystic, made the following comments about sacrifice:

I am fully persuaded of His designs toward you, as well for the sanctification of others, as for your own sanctification.

Let me assure you, this is not attained, save through pain, weariness and labor, and it will be reached by a path that will wonderfully disappoint your expectations. Nevertheless, if you are fully convinced that it is on the nothing in man that God establishes his greatest works,—you will be in part guarded against disappointment or surprise. He destroys that He might build; for when He is about to rear his sacred temple in us, he first totally razes that vain and pompous edifice, which human art and power had erected, and from its horrible ruins a new structure is formed, by His power only. (Guyon, 2006)

Before I continue, it is necessary for me to explain how I use the term "greatness" within the context of this text. Greatness may be defined as (1) superior in quality or importance; (2) powerful, influential; (3) distinguished; (4) of outstanding significance or importance; and/or (5) remarkable or outstanding in magnitude, degree, or extent (American Heritage Dictionary, 2011).

Adding to this definition, I would describe greatness as an individual exhibiting superior qualities in his/her said profession so much so that it distinguishes them from others in that specific field or arena. This individual realizes that he/she is not competing with others per se but rather competing with himself or herself to be the best at what he/she was designed, created, or purposed to do.

I have come to realize that the concept or perception of greatness varies from individual to individual. Thus, one cannot and should not impose one's idea or notion of greatness onto someone else nor should anyone cajole or even force someone to be in a place where they are not ready to be or don't desire to be, a mistake that many of us have made throughout the course of our lives.

Each of us is on a journey, a journey to greatness, a journey to your own "promised land," a journey that will require you to explore territories that have not been discovered or explored before. A journey can be described as a long and often difficult process of personal change and development (Journey, n.d.). I add to this description—a long and sometimes difficult, yet rewarding, process of personal change and development in the fulfillment of purpose. Your greatness is embodied in your purpose.

Each of us was born with a unique purpose to fulfill; however, each of our paths in the fulfillment of purpose is different but will have some similarities. Each path has been specifically tailor-made with you in mind (Trimm, 2011). In order to accomplish this God-given purpose, we must take a journey into what appears to be "unexplored territory." Oftentimes, we are given a glimpse as to some great things that we will do or accomplish during our lifetime. Some of us have envisioned ourselves as entrepreneurs, astronauts, engineers, pastors, motivational speakers, lawyer, teachers, doctors, and even authors. Whatever the vision that God has given you, you must know that the journey you take will equip and prepare you for your ultimate position in life.

Let your mind start a journey thru a strange
new world. Leave all thoughts of the world you

knew before. Let your soul take you where you
long to be…Close your eyes let your spirit start
to soar and you'll live as you've never lived before.
(Fromm, n.d.)

On this journey, you will encounter trepidation, doubt, hope-
lessness, insecurities, and much more. Don't let these "building
blocks" of life deter you from pursuing and accomplishing your
purpose, but, rather, let them build the Godly character that you
will need to sustain you as you transition from one stage to the next
throughout your journey.

If all difficulties were known at the outset of
a long journey, most of us would never start out
at all. (Rather, n.d.)

At some point in our lives, we have all felt that "there is more to
life than this. Something is missing. There is a void in my life." We
attend church on a regular basis, assume leadership positions, have
good jobs, make good money, and commit our lives to a lifetime of
service, and yet we realize there is something more to life than what we
are experiencing now. In the movie, *The Matrix*, the character, Neo,
is torn between two worlds: one that he has become accustomed to
and one that offered the unimaginable—to fulfill that which he was
born to do. He did not know what lay ahead, and yet he had to make
a choice. The character, Trinity, made the following statement to Neo:

Because you have been down there Neo,
you know that road, you know exactly where it

ends. And I know that's not where you want to
be. (Trinity, *The Matrix*)

Now, I am sure you are wondering why I chose this particular
line to help me convey what many of us feel when we have to make
decisions that can alter the course of our life. Neo had to decide
whether to continue with life as he knew it to be or to find out just
how "deep the rabbit hole goes." There would be no turning back.
My point here is that at some point, you will have to make a decision
to continue with life as you have known it to be or choose the road of
unchartered territory. Once you make the choice, how you navigate
your individual journey will greatly depend on your ability to follow God's internal Global Positioning System designed and imparted
into the life of every believer to assist in navigating life's challenges in
pursuit and the fulfillment of purpose. Again, the choice you make
will require a sacrifice. This choice will require a sacrifice of your will,
old habits, and former paradigms. But the reward is worth it. It will
not be easy, but it will be worth it.

Throughout this book, I would like for you to view yourselves
as *data collectors*. In educational research, a data collector is one who
is engaged in the process of collecting and analyzing data based on
a set of predefined or predetermined variables in an established sys-
tematic fashion that enables one to answer questions and possibly
draw conclusions or rather correlations. Within the context of this
text, a data collector is one who is engaged in collecting data that will
eventually be used for future purposes. The data you collect will serve
as the spiritual muscles you will need as you continue throughout
your life's journey. You will collect a wealth of data to include your
successes and failures, your ups and your downs, your feelings of

rejection and abandonment, and your disappointments, insecurities, fears, what makes you cry, what makes you laugh, and what makes you happy. As you travel throughout your journey, realize that the Holy Spirit is with you even if he doesn't appear to be.

I am of the persuasion that *most* things in life happen for a reason, and therefore it is imperative that we are cognizant of everything that is happening in our sphere. In their book, *Super Brain*, Chopra and Tanzi (2012) describe this phenomenon of awareness as paying attention to the stream of input and selecting, deciding, sorting, processing, and making choices about what to do with that input. Remember, you are *data collectors*. Now, in the context of their book, they are talking about how to effectively transform your brain into what they call a "super brain." However, I want you from this point forward to consciously take note of everything that happens in your life even, the minutest detail, as building blocks in the attainment of your personal greatness. Ask the Holy Spirit to help you in this process. Get a journal and take note of these experiences and reflect on them. It may not make sense now, but as my elders used to say, you will understand it better by and by.

I conceptualize this text as being one that incites a purposeful journey, one in which the journeyer is purposefully engaged every step of the way allowing the Holy Spirit to guide them through every triumph, every disappointment, every rejection, every failure, every success. As you maneuver throughout your journey, you will discover a lot about yourself including your likes and dislikes, shortcomings, strengths, and weaknesses. You must be open to these findings. You have to be willing to not only accept the good things about yourself, but you have to be willing to face the not so good things as well. Failure to do so could hinder how well you navigate your course. If you fail to acknowledge the fact that you are a "slacker" and lack diligence, then you will not be able to counteract these through things such as goal setting and time management.

I used to think that bad situations or choices served to undermine God's will for my life. I thought that greatness was some far-fetched idea reserved for someone else. It was not until later in my adulthood that I realized that I had significance, that I too had greatness inside me. I realized that I was living in the narrowed expectations and opinions that I allowed others to place on me. I allowed others to put limitations on my life. I asked questions that are familiar to most. Why did I have to go through this particular situation? Why did I get this life? Why wasn't I graced with long locks and she does? Why do I have pimples and they don't? Why do we have to struggle and they do not? How come they have all of the money and we do not? Was God biased? My questions were never ending. No one had the answers, or they did not have answers that made sense to me. I had done everything I was supposed to do and was still unfulfilled. Something was missing.

When I graduated from college, I began to question God about all of the "ills" and "woes" of my life. At this time, I was teaching school and working part-time at an electronics store. One day, a gentleman walked into the store looking for some item. I began to assist him, and, somehow, we started a conversation about God. He proceeded to ask me if I "knew" the Holy Spirit. Of course, I said. He asked me this question again. I thought more and realized that he was asking me something a bit deeper. He was asking me about my relationship with the Holy Spirit. I realized that I was clueless. My relationship with the Holy Spirit was superficial. I had a knowledge of him by way of scripture only. I continued to study the Bible and pray, but I began to simply spend time in his presence not necessarily looking for anything other than to know him. I worshipped and talked to him almost daily. This was a wonderful time, but it was also very frustrating. I started reading books by famous ministers and their encounter with the Holy Spirit. And here I was again, allowing others' experiences to dictate how my relationship with him should be. I am a firm believer that he relates to us based on our own uniqueness. He is not looking for perfection. He is looking for relationship. He wants to fill the voids in our lives. He wants to help you to become your best self. This is neither a quick process nor is it an easy one. You will be frustrated and at times stretched beyond measure.

Odd, how life makes twists and turns. I never would have guessed that I'd end up where I am now, but I wouldn't trade it for the world. I wouldn't trade this path I'm on for the whole solar system, for that matter. If I've learned anything these last several months, it's that sometimes the most scenic roads in life are the detours you didn't mean to take. (Angela N. Blount, *Once Upon an Ever After*)

You will traverse through difficult terrain as you journey through your wilderness into your promised land. Let us take this journey together. Make the choice to start your purposeful journey acknowledging and allowing the Holy Spirit to guide you into unchartered territory. The choice is yours.

Several years ago, Robert Frost wrote a poem entitled, *The Road Not Taken*. Many people, without truly reading the poem, assume that this poem depicts a road not traveled by many; however, closer analysis of this poem reveals that there in fact is no road that is less traveled but rather a choice to be made by the traveler about which road to take. Both roads in Frost's poem had been well traveled. The traveler simply had to make a choice.

> *Two roads diverged in a yellow wood*
> *And sorry I could not travel both*
> *And be one traveler, long I stood*
> *And looked down one as far as I could*
> *To where it bent in the undergrowth;*
> *Then took the other, as just as fair*
> *And having perhaps the better claim,*
> *Because it was grassy and wanted wear;*
> *Though as for that, the passing there*
> *Had worn them really about the same,*
> *And both that morning equally lay*
> *In leaves no step had trodden black.*
> *Oh, I kept the first for another day!*
> *Yet knowing how way leads on to way,*
> *I doubted if I should ever come back.*
> *I shall be telling this with a sigh*
> *Somewhere ages and ages hence:*
> *Two roads diverged in a wood and I—*
> *I took the one less traveled by,*
> *And that has made all the difference.*

Pearls of Wisdom #1. Make the choice to start your purposeful journey by acknowledging and allowing the Holy Spirit to guide you into unchartered territory.

Pearls of Wisdom #2. Remember, you are data collectors in your journey. Be cognizant of the things, people, and situations that you encounter along your journey. Ask the Holy Spirit to help you in this process. Get a journal and take note of these experiences and reflect on them. These learning experiences are the building blocks in the attainment of your personal greatness. Ask yourself the question, what are my takeaways?

Chapter 1

TO BOLDLY GO:
THE CHOICE IS YOURS!

Life, in and of itself, is a journey. You have a
choice—you can passively engage the journey and
let life pass you by, or you can actively engage your
journey and YOU can happen to life and life
can happen for you!! (Donna P. Turner, PhD)

If you have ever taken a trip, then you know the preparation that went into planning that trip. For those who are serious planners, preparation most likely started weeks or months prior to the trip. Once the decision has been made to take a trip, several things must be considered: you must determine the destination, mode of travel, places to visit when you get there, items to take on the trip, and the journey back home. If the mode of travel is by car, then most people will use a GPS to ensure that they get to their destination in the fastest and most efficient manner. Most likely, there is more than one route to that one destination, and, surely, there are different modes of transportation; however, it is up to the individual to choose the path since the GPS will not choose it for you. The journey of life is no different. We set a destination and choose the path we believe that will take us there as quickly as possible with no detours. Life's journey is not that simple. As we travel along life's journey, we experience a number of successes, disappointments, detours, and challenges. As I previously mentioned, our varied experiences are the building blocks of life and help to prepare for the next phase of our journey.

My parents divorced when I was around five or six years old. I remember it vividly. Those were some of my roughest years. My mom cried a lot while she struggled to raise three young children in the South where racism was overt and prevalent. My sister and I visited my dad on the weekends, and during the summer, he would take us to Six Flags over Georgia. Those trips with my dad were the highlight of my summer. My aunt and uncle, who were like a second mom and dad to me, were very loving and very supportive of our family. My mom taught me strength, and my aunt taught me how to be a young lady. Although I had a good support system, I was unhappy with my lot in life. I struggled with low self-esteem and insecurity and always sought affirmation from others. I was the "good girl" and chose to be the "good girl" because I wanted to be liked by my teachers and peers. I fantasized about a different life, a different story, not realizing that I had the innate ability to write my own.

If you care about what people think about
you, you will end up being their slave. Reject and
pull your own rope. (Auliq Ice, 2017)

I was always intrigued with God. I went to church and read the Bible often, even though I didn't always understand what I was reading. When I was twelve, I gave my life to Christ. It was my decision, and my mother had no idea of my intention. It is difficult to articulate what prompted me to do this, but I now realize that God's Spirit was already at work within me. I continued to fantasize about a different life, a different story, because I simply was not satisfied with the one I had. I was too young and naive to realize that everything that I was experiencing was preparing me for the next phase of my journey. Trust me, I know that many twelve-year-olds are not sitting around thinking about how their mistakes are preparing them for life's journey.

My fourteen-year-old daughter could care less about a journey. She is only concerned about the next football game, the next dance, and boys. However, when she is faced with difficult situations that require her to make choices, it is my job to *assist* her with thinking about the pros and cons of each choice and to be comfortable with the outcome. Children make choices daily, and they too need to understand the consequences of the choices they make and how it could impact their lives.

I am sure that many of us have felt confused and overwhelmed as to what path we should have pursued at various stages of life's journey, and I am also sure that the anxiety experienced weighed heavily on the psyche as we endeavored to make sure that we were on the right track in our desire to please God and fulfill his purpose. The beauty in choosing the "right" path or making the "right" decision or even choosing the "wrong" path or making the "wrong" decision is that God is everywhere, at all times, and ready to guide us throughout this arduous yet very rewarding journey. Even if we make a choice that leads to unfavorable conditions, God will help us to get back on course, that is, if we allow.

Do you recall Frost's poem, "The Road Not Taken"? The *traveler* had to make a choice not knowing what lies ahead. I can only assume that he had a destination in mind as he was contemplating which path to take. He comments, "Oh, I kept the first for another day! Yet knowing how way leads on to way, I doubted if I should ever come back." In other words, the traveler determined that he could simply take the road not chosen another day even though he knew in himself that he may not ever come that way again. The traveler made a choice and accepted the notion that he may not ever be able to go down the path not chosen.

The average adult makes thousands of choices each day, intentional or not. What do I want to be when I grow up (I asked myself this question when I was thirty)? Do I want to go to college? What college should I attend? Do I want to get married? Do I want to have children? These are choices that we make at some point during our journey; however, there are numerous choices that we make throughout our day. What am I going to wear today (I am contemplating this as I type)? What am I going to eat for breakfast? Lunch? Dinner? Should I attend a 9:00 a.m. meeting at church? Should I reward my daughter for good grades today by taking her to her favorite ice cream parlor? There are hundreds of choices that I will make today without much thought; however, a few will require more contemplation than others. In other words, I will have to consider the ramifications or consequences of the choices that I will make, but I must make a choice.

Life's choices can be a bit scary, and if you have had your share of ups and downs, you may be apprehensive when having to make a choice that could impact your norm. Life's experiences impact the way we decide to engage life and our willingness to take chances. For some, one bad relationship was the deciding factor as to whether or not you chose to get married. For others, one rejection letter from the human resources officer at our dream job could lead to settling for a position at a company that you never wanted to work for. Life happens to all. There is a consequence, good or bad, for every choice we make; but we *must* make a choice. Even if we choose not to make a choice, we have made a choice to do nothing, and there is a consequence for that as well.

Some people truly embody the phrase made famous by Nike, "Just Do It," while others, like myself, have had to constantly profess that, "I can do it." Why is it that some people seem to have been graced with a natural capacity to accomplish whatever they set their minds to do, even if it means failure, while some people have to be convinced and cajoled into believing and knowing that they too are called to do some great thing and that they too can do it?

Everyone desires to do some great or notable work, but many are simply scared to fail. Some have a desire to own their own business, and some have a desire to travel the world but refuse to take the steps that their dreams will not become realized because they fear failure. Some people will allow failure to become a steppingstone to success while others allow failure to paralyze and incapacitate their dreams forever. Where do you fall on this continuum?

Every decision that we make in life has a consequence. If our bad decision leads to unfavorable consequences, ideally, we should not allow those consequences to paralyze us; however, oftentimes we do. It is OK if we allow our failures, disappointments, or fears to temporarily incapacitate us; however, we must refuse to dwell in that place for too long. Failures, disappointments, and fears can serve our greater good if we permit them too. Our stations in life are not stagnant or fixed. We have the capacity to change our stations in life by simply choosing a different path or course or finding a different strategy to accomplish the goals that we have set for ourselves. We must be sure to glean all that we can from every place that we find ourselves, good or bad. Information taken from every phase of our journey allows us to become a better-informed person and able to assist others facing the same trial or dilemma along the way. The idea is to acknowledge God in every endeavor so that he can assist you in charting your journey. I believe that we are indeed the "author of our individual life story." God has placed everything we need inside of us.

> According as his divine power hath given unto us all things that pertain unto life and godliness, through the knowledge of him that hath called us to glory and virtue. (2 Peter 1:3, KJV)

Not only has God placed everything we need to create the life that we want to live, he has given us a teacher to guide us along a life's journey.

> But the Comforter, which is the Holy Ghost, whom the Father will send in my name, he shall teach you all things, and bring all things to your remembrance, whatsoever I have said unto you. (John 14:26, KJV)

You will encounter difficulties that almost seem to exhaust you in every way possible. The challenge is to know that God is with you every step of the way even when it appears as though he is missing in action. Remember, he said that he would never leave us or forsake us although we oftentimes leave and forsake him. We must learn to trust him, wait on him, and acknowledge him in *everything* we do. There is no place on Earth we can go where God does not know our whereabouts. There is not one bad decision that we can make and God not have an alternate road that will get us back on course.

> Your journey has molded you for your greater good, and it was exactly what it needed to be. Don't think you've lost time. There is no short-cutting to life. It took each and every situation you have encountered to bring you to the now. And now is right on time. (Asha Tyson, 2001)

How many times have you reflected over your life and thought to yourself that somewhere you made a "wrong turn" or you simply "lost your way" and did not know where or how to pick up the pieces and start again? You were an emotional wreck, and yet somehow you found the motivation to keep going although you had no idea where you were going next. As I reflect on those moments when I was in what I called "idiotville" because that is just what I felt like—an idiot—each time I chose what I thought was the wrong path or made a bad decision, I realized that it was that bad decisions and/or that wrong path that built character and integrity and taught me about the importance of trusting the leading of the Holy Spirit every step of the way.

> Sometimes you have to ride over the bumps in the road to avoid running off a cliff. Other times you may have to fall into the potholes to avoid hitting the trees. Some days you have to experience the wrong turns, to recognize the right ones. There is no better navigation system than bad experiences in life so that we can recalculate our lives through better choices to reach our intended destination. (Eugene Nathaniel Butler, Retrieved August 2015)

> You can never regret anything you do in life. You kind of have to learn the lesson from whatever the experience is and take it with you on your journey forward. (Aubrey O'Day, Retrieved August 2015)

Humanity has done a phenomenal job in creating a navigational system that is able to pinpoint an object's location at any point on Earth at any given time through satellite signals. However, this particular system can only provide the directions for an already determined destination. It cannot choose for you. You must set the destination, and this system will provide a direct route as well as alternate routes to assist you in getting to your destination in a timely manner with as few obstacles (i.e., tolls, road work, etc.) as possible. This system, the GPS, has the capacity to (1) determine the exact location of person or a vehicle anywhere in the world; (2) determine the shortest distance between two places; (3) find objects in the dark or in unfamiliar territory; (4) enable researchers to explore the Earth's environment including the atmosphere and gravity field; and (5) allow for ecological studies such as animal tracking and behavior.

In God's GPS, God monitors life's journey through the Holy Spirit. He constantly and consistently encircles and watches over us. He knows our exact location, position, and velocity at all times. The term "location" is used to identify a specific point or area on the Earth's surface. In other words, God is able to determine our exact location at any given moment in time. This idea of location is beautifully illustrated in Psalm 139:7–12. Meditate on these verses using the King James Version and the Message Bible.

> Whither shall I go from thy spirit? Or whither shall I flee from thy presence? If I ascend up into heaven, thou art there: if I make my bed in hell, behold, thou art there. If I take the wings of the morning, and dwell in the uttermost parts of the sea. Even there shall thy hand lead me, and thy right hand shall hold me. If I say, Surely the darkness shall cover me; even the night shall be light about me. Yea, the darkness hideth not from thee; but the night shineth as the day: the darkness and the light are both alike to thee. (Psalm 139:7–12, KJV)

> Is there any place I can go to avoid your Spirit? to be out of your sight? If I climb to the sky,

you're there! If I go underground, you're there! If I flew on morning's wings to the far western horizon, You'd find me in a minute—you're already there waiting! Then I said to myself, "Oh, he even sees me in the dark! At night I'm immersed in the light!" It's a fact: darkness isn't dark to you; night and day, darkness and light, they're all the same to you. (Psalm 139:7–12, Message Bible)

Psalms 139 provides a magnificent yet detailed account of the omniscience or all-knowing capacity of God. The term "omniscience" can be defined as the capacity to know everything that there is to know (Oxford English Dictionary, 2005).

There is no place on Earth that we can go or even hide where God will not know our exact whereabouts. He is everywhere present at all times. God takes austere notice of every step we take whether right or wrong. He knows what rule we walk by, what end we walk toward, and even the very company we keep (Matthew Henry Commentary, 1997).

You are not on a journey to God; you are on a journey WITH God. (Steve Maraboli)

I am no longer afraid of becoming lost, because the journey back always reveals something new, and that is ultimately good for the artist. (Billy Joel, 2014)

The term "position" describes a situation or condition relative to a specific place or location especially with relation to favorable or unfavorable conditions (Dictionary.com, n.d.). God knows our exact state or position, favorable or unfavorable, at all times. This should be comforting; however, if you are like me, it can also be a bit unnerving. I, like many of you, have been in some very challenging, difficult, precarious, frustrating, testing, and frightening situations throughout my life. I know that I used several adjectives to describe my various states of being at different points in my life, but that is exactly how I felt. Oftentimes, I was overwhelmed with life and "bad" choices. It was not until later in my Christian walk that I realized that every emotion experienced, every good and bad decision, and every "alternative" path traveled were designed to teach me to lean on and trust the guidance of the Holy Spirit in everything I do. It is impossible to *always* choose the "right" path or make the "best" decision in life. Sometimes it is the wrong path and the worst decisions that serve as the building blocks of life that facilitate the development of the knowledge and wisdom needed to gracefully maneuver you throughout the remainder of your journey. It is the difficult situations that yield some of the best rewards.

The term "velocity" is a significant part of one's journey. In layman's terms, velocity describes distance, speed, and direction (retrieved from http://www.physicsclassroom.com/class/1DKin/Lesson-1/Speed-and-Velocity).

God knows our posture, our perspective, and our state of being relative to where we are at any stage of our journey. He knows what direction we are traveling, and he knows how long it will take us to get there. He also knows when we are trying to get to a specific destination too fast. Remember, it is all about timing—no need to rush—enjoy the moment.

At one point in my journey, I was facing a divorce. This was a weighty decision and something I did not take lightly. I prayed and asked for guidance. I had to consider the consequences of my choice. Could I truly make it on my own? How would this affect my daughter? What would my family say? What would his family say? What would the church folks say? And let's not forget about the image that I had worked so hard to build and protect that was crumbling before me. I had a lovely home, drove a nice car, was an elder in my church, and was living what I thought to be the *American dream*. My feelings were the last to be considered. However, I had come to a place where I had to be honest with myself. I was unhappy. I was unhappy with myself and with the image I had created. Well, none of this surprised God. He knew my state of mind. He knew where I was in my thinking, and he knew the path I would eventually choose. He also knew what lie ahead. He knew when I was angry, hurt, perplexed, frustrated, overwhelmed, and unsure of this unfamiliar and extremely difficult place in my life. But greater still, he also knew the time frame that it would take to go through the process of this phase of the journey. Again, velocity describes speed and direction.

Thus, God knows the various paths or direction that we will choose at various stages of our journey, and he also knows how long it will take us to get there. The problem, however, with many of us is that we don't ask God for insight regarding our journey. Many of us have embraced a song made popular by Frank Sinatra and later Elvis Presley entitled, "My Way." Please don't get me wrong, I am actually a fan of this song; however, the point I would like to make here is that many Christians are doing it "their way" without any regard for the Holy Spirit. We make plans, but we don't include Holy Spirit. Believe it or not, the Holy Spirit wants to be a part of everything we do. I try to consult with him about everything—relationships, career, and education.

The relationship that I have with God's Holy Spirit is not a relationship that happened overnight. It was and still is a process, one that requires time and patience. It will require time, effort, and sacrifice on your part if you truly want to know him. I am a bit resolute and at times "hardheaded." In addition to my resolute and obstinate ways, I am a thinker. I have to process everything. Now, I operate in faith, and I have learned to trust the leading of the Holy Spirit in all that I do. Is it still challenging at times? Absolutely!

Someone once asked me, "What did you do when you had to make a life-changing decision in resigning from your previous job?"

I thought about it for a moment. I wanted to say something really profound, but I had to be completely honest about what I experienced during my decision-making process. I had been teaching for fifteen years and was completely burnt out. I no longer wanted to teach, but I was terrified about leaving my position. While I was no longer happy with my teaching assignment, it provided a steady income. I was married and had a small child, so I had to think about the consequences of my decision. So when faced with the decision as to stay with a job that I was unhappy with or to resign and trust God to provide for us, this is what I did. I closed my eyes and jumped off the cliff into unknown possibilities and told the Holy Spirit that if my jump into the unknown resulted in a mess, then please clean up after me. I quit and never looked back. It was truly a leap of faith, one that I have never experienced before. This was a very scary time in my life, but I did not have any regrets. I learned to trust God a little at a time. You see, trust is a choice, and with each difficult decision, you have to decide whether or not to trust God.

> For me, doing the actual work to fulfill the vision is the easy part. It's the emotional journey that I go through as I am free falling into the unknown that is the hard part. But each time I jump, I'm learning to trust that God will continue to guide me and help me to land safely. (Yvonne Pierre, *The Day My Soul Cried: A Memoir*)

> We must cease striving and trust God to provide what He thinks is best and in whatever time He chooses to make it available. But this kind of trusting doesn't come naturally. It's a spiritual crisis of the will in which we must choose to exercise faith. (Charles R. Swindoll)

I want to call your attention to a familiar passage of scripture:

> And Jesus being full of the Holy Ghost returned from Jordan, and was led by the Spirit into the wilderness, Being forty days tempted of the devil. And in those days he did eat nothing: and when they were ended, he afterward hungered. And the devil said unto him, If thou be the Son of God, command this stone that it be made bread. And Jesus answered him, saying, It

is written, That man shall not live by bread alone, but by every word of God. And the devil, taking him up into an high mountain, shewed unto him all the kingdoms of the world in a moment of time. And the devil said unto him, All this power will I give thee, and the glory of them: for that is delivered unto me; and to whomsoever I will I give it. If thou therefore wilt worship me, all shall be thine. And Jesus answered and said unto him, Get thee behind me, Satan: for it is written, Thou shalt worship the Lord thy God, and him only shalt thou serve...And when the devil had ended all the temptation, he departed from him for a season. And Jesus returned in the power of the Spirit into Galilee: and there went out a fame of him through all the region round about... And there was delivered unto him the book of the prophet Esaias. And when he had opened the book, he found the place where it was written, The Spirit of the Lord is upon me, because he hath anointed me to preach the gospel to the poor; he hath sent me to heal the brokenhearted, to preach deliverance to the captives, and recovering of sight to the blind, to set at liberty them that are bruised. (Luke 4:1–8, 13, 14, 17, 18)

There are several different points that can be engaged from studying this passage of scripture; however, I would like to highlight one point in particular. In Luke 4:1, notice who was leading Jesus into the wilderness—the Holy Spirit. Jesus had just returned from the Jordan where he was baptized by John the Baptist.

> And Jesus, when he was baptized, went up straightway out of the water: and, lo, the heavens were opened unto him, and he saw the Spirit of God descending like a dove, and lighting upon him: And lo a voice from heaven, saying, This is my beloved Son, in whom I am well pleased. (Matthew 3:16–17)

Jesus was affirmed by the Father who said, "This is my Beloved Son, in whom I am well pleased." Now, it is not my desire to engage in textual criticism at this juncture in order to deal with all of the nuances of this passage but rather to see how it relates to the life of the believer in this present age. It is rather difficult to imagine such a loving Father who affirms his love for his Son and furthermore expresses his adulation for his obedience, to lead him into the "wilderness" to be tempted of the devil (v.1). The Greek translation for the term "led" is *egeto* which means to bring, carry, or guide (Strong, 1990). The Greek translation for "wilderness" is *eremo* which describes a desert or solitary place (Strong, 1990). Thus, the wilderness that Jesus was *led* to was a deserted, abandoned waste land.

Again, it is hard to imagine that a loving Father would lead his beloved Son into an abandoned place where he knew the temptations that lie ahead. However, God, who is omniscient, knew the path that Jesus took. He also knew the result of the Messiah's "wilderness experience." He knew that it was necessary even expedient that Jesus engage his wilderness experience for the greater mission that lies ahead. You see, this "wilderness experience" was a part of Jesus's preparation for ministry. The passage clearly indicates that the purpose of Jesus being led into the wilderness was to be tempted. The Greek term for "tempted," *peirazomenos*, means to make proof of, attempt, or test (Strong, 1990). Jesus was tempted in every area of life—lust of the flesh, lust of the eyes, and pride of life.

> For all that is in the world, the lust of the flesh, and the lust of the eyes, and the pride of life, is not of the Father, but is of the world. (1 John 2:16)

In *Matthew Henry's Commentary*, the "lust of the flesh" is described as the appetite of indulging fleshly pleasures and, objectively, all those things that excite and inflame the pleasures of the flesh. The eyes are described as being delighted with treasures and suggest that riches and rich possessions are craved by an extravagant eye, which is the lust of covetousness. Lastly, the pride of life is described as a vain mind that craves all the grandeur, equipage, and pomp of a vain-glorious life. It is the ambition and thirst of honor and applause. In the same manner that God knew what lies ahead for Jesus, he also knows what trials, temptations, and challenges lie ahead for us. These challenges and temptations were simply permitted to equip us with the tools that we would need throughout our journey in the fulfillment of purpose.

It is important that we understand that God does not have a problem with material things or pleasures because these were created for our enjoyment; however, the problem comes when we substitute a love or lust for things, money, or the pomp of a vain-glorious life for God. God uses every detail of our journey to prepare us for the purpose to which each of us is called. Every journey is different, and every situation is unique because the individual experiencing the journey is unique, although the process and the emotions experienced are similar. The manner in which we handle, or process, life is based on our unique physical, emotional, and psychological makeup.

Another unique aspect of God's GPS is the capacity of the Holy Spirit to monitor our health and our wellbeing. So not only does the Holy Spirit determine our position, location, and velocity, he also monitors how efficient we are in our daily life matters.

> The spirit of man is the candle of the Lord searching all the inward parts of the belly. (Proverbs 20:27)
>
> The spirit of man [that factor in human personality which proceeds immediately from God] is the lamp of the Lord, searching all His innermost parts. (Proverbs 20:27, Amplified)

Matthew Henry's Commentary says that:

> The spirit of a man has a self-consciousness; it searches into the dispositions and affections of the soul, praises what is good, condemns what is otherwise, and judges of the thoughts and intents of the heart. This is the office, this is the power, of conscience, which we are therefore concerned to get rightly informed and to keep void of offence.

He monitors our health and our efficiency regarding our jobs, family, education, relationships, and much more. He monitors our state of mind before determining if we are indeed ready to transition to our next destination. In 2000, I applied for a doctoral program in science education at a prestigious university. I had just completed an educational specialist program at another university with a 3.8 grade point average. Surely, I thought I would be accepted. I prayed, of course, and thought that this was the will of God and the perfect timing. Needless to say, I did not get accepted into the program. I was crushed when I read the opening sentence, "Thank you for your interest, but unfortunately, we cannot accept you." I cried, pouted, and was angry with God. At the time, I was a high school science teacher and felt as though my time at my current school had come to an end, so I thought. Since I could not start the doctoral program, I began to apply for other jobs. I applied everywhere; I was simply tired of teaching at the secondary level. I received one rejection letter after the other. I cried every day. I asked God what he wanted me to do. I was hurt and confused. To make it worse, it seemed as though I was constantly confronted with individuals younger than me who were working on their PhDs. I thought this was *very* unfair. I had no idea as to what God wanted me to do, so I waited. I continued to teach and work in the ministry. It would be approximately seven years later before I would be accepted into the same doctoral program at the university that had previously turned me down. These events are quite interesting.

In 2007, I started working on my doctorate. In 2008, I was offered a Graduate Research Assistantship (GRA) that would pay for my tuition and provide a small monthly stipend. My then advisor had just received a multimillion-dollar grant, and I would be hired as a GRA to work under this grant. As I mentioned earlier, I resigned from my teaching job and never looked back. As a GRA, I acquired knowledge and skills that I could have never gained as a part-time doctoral student. God knew this. He knew what lies ahead, and so he waited until the timing was right before he opened the door for me to take this position. I assumed that when I applied to the program in 2000, "no" meant never. That was not the case. I knew I wanted to get my PhD, and I knew where I wanted to attend school. My interpretation of the timing of what I believed God to be suggesting was off. Again, God knew a better and more rewarding opportunity lies ahead. Remember, God also monitors our overall health, efficiency, and mental state of being. He knew that I was not ready for the doctoral program because of the number of challenges that I would be confronted with. For example, I was insecure about my ability to write and do presentations, all of which are an important part of the program. I was also concerned that I would not finish the program. To be quite honest, my fleeting thought was to get through the course work and drop out when it came time to research and defend my dissertation. I have to say at this point that God is not only loving, but he is strategic in all that he does.

When I started the GRA position, I learned to collect data through observations and interviews, and I learned how to conduct basic analyses using a statistical software package called the Statistical Package for the Social Sciences (SPSS). Needless to say, that by the time I was ready to do the data collection component of my dissertation and defend, I was ready.

But I trusted in, relied on, *and* was confident in You, O Lord; I said, You are my God.

My times are in Your hands. (Psalm 31:14–15a, Amplified)

To everything there is a season, and a time for every matter *or* purpose under heaven: A time to be born and a time to die, a time to plant and a time to pluck up what is planted, A time to kill and a time to heal, a time to break down and a time to build up, A time to weep and a time to laugh, a time to mourn and a time to dance, A time to cast away stones and a time to gather stones together, a time to embrace and a time to refrain from embracing, A time to get and a time to lose, a time to keep and a time to cast away, A time to rend and a time to sew, a time to keep silence and a time to speak, A time to love and a time to hate, a time for war and a time for peace. (Ecclesiastes 3:1–8)

It is about timing, our state of being, and our capacity to handle the next phase or position of the journey. These are the things that the Holy Spirit is constantly monitoring throughout our journey.

Again, the Holy Spirit acts as God's GPS in the life of every believer. He determines our location, our position, and our velocity. He monitors our well-being and our readiness to engage the next phase of our journey. The Holy Spirit is the conduit by which God communicates with us and assists in navigating our journey.

Guidance, like all God's acts of blessing under the covenant of grace, is a sovereign act.

Not merely does God will to guide us in the sense of showing us his way, that we may tread it; he wills also to guide us in the more fundamental sense of ensuring that, whatever happens, whatever mistakes we may make, we shall come safely home. Slippings and strayings there will be, no doubt, but the everlasting arms are beneath us; we shall be caught, rescued, restored. This is God's promise; this is how good he is. (Packer, 1993)

It is up to the believer to make full use of God's GPS. When I first started using a GPS, it took me some time to understand all of the functions of this device. I had to learn how to program it, and I had to familiarize myself with its capabilities. One aspect of the GPS that I loved was the notion that whenever I got off course or could not find my intended destination because a new subdivision or business was not recognized by the GPS, I could always press the icon for home, and the GPS would immediately guide me back to my starting point.

The succeeding chapters will illuminate how the Holy Spirit strategically, gracefully, and compassionately guides us through the highs and lows of life, helping us to acquire the knowledge and skills and spiritual fortitude we need to navigate life's journey. Remember, you are data collectors along life's journey. There is nothing insignificant about your journey. Everything counts down to the smallest detail. Take nothing for granted. Ask the Holy Spirit to heighten your senses, making you cognizant of everything in your sphere. But I must warn you that while you are traveling on your journey, it is imperative that you remain alert and cognizant as to those things or people that can serve as a distraction or a signal blocker incapacitating or numbing your communication and tracking system between you and the Holy Spirit. Now, I am not referring to the situations or people that you must glean from at times but rather those that can distort or block your communication system during your journey.

A GPS receiver requires a line of sight to the satellites in order to obtain a signal representative of the exact location of the object of interest or of the individual using the GPS receiver. When a receiver cannot receive signals from the satellite, then the communication between the satellite and the receiver is lost, resulting in the message, "GPS Signal Lost." Thus, a signal blocker is any obstacle that prevents proper communication between the GPS and satellite. Signal blockers in the life of the believer can be distractions that distort or block communication between the believer and the Holy Spirit. These blockers or distractions can prevent you from hearing what the Holy Spirit is attempting to convey to you, or there simply may be too much noise interference distorting what is actually being said.

And when the woman saw that the tree was good for food, and that it was pleasant to the eyes, and a tree to be desired to make one wise, she took of the fruit thereof, and did eat, and gave also unto her husband with her; and he did eat. And the eyes of them both were opened, and they knew that they were naked; and they sewed fig leaves together and made themselves aprons. And they heard the voice of the LORD God walking in the garden in the cool of the day: and Adam and his wife hid themselves from the presence of the LORD God amongst the trees of the garden. And the LORD God called unto Adam, and said unto him, Where art thou? And he said, I heard thy voice in the garden, and I was afraid, because I was naked; and I hid myself. And he said, Who told thee that thou wast naked? Hast thou eaten of the tree, whereof I commanded thee that thou shouldest not eat? (Genesis 3:6–11, KJV)

Prior to the events in Genesis chapter 3, Adam communed with God daily. God entrusted to Adam his template as to how his kingdom should be established in Earth.

And God said, Let us make man in our image, after our likeness: and let them have dominion over the fish of the sea, and over the fowl of the air, and over the cattle, and over all the earth, and over every creeping thing that creepeth upon the earth. So God created man in his own image, in the image of God created he him; male and female created he them. And God blessed them, and God said unto them, Be fruitful, and multiply, and replenish the earth, and subdue it: and have dominion over the fish of the sea, and over the fowl of the air, and over every living thing that moveth upon the earth. (Genesis 1:26–28, KJV)

It was God's plan for Adam to have complete authority over the Earth and its constituents. Adam was to completely subdue the Earth using all of its resources in the service of God and man (Genesis 1:28, Amp). However, something thwarted or frustrated God's plan for man on Earth. The lines of communication between Adam and God were now distorted. Pride and disobedience ushered in sin, and now Adam found himself "hiding" from the presence of God. The Hebrew term for "hide" is *chaba* which means to withdraw or conceal (Strong, 1990). The Hebrew term for "presence" is *paniym* and can be translated as "face," implying a close and personal encounter with the Lord (Strong, 1990). Thus, Adam allowed sin to sever the communication lines between him and God. Pride and disobedience in this context were the signal blockers that severed the lines of communication between God and man.

Again, it is vitally important that you are cognizant of those signal blockers that can distort or sever the communication between you and the Holy Spirit, thereby preventing you from getting the strategies and direction you need for each step along your journey. Let the Holy Spirit assist in what needs to be filtered and what needs to be filed away. Let us continue by examining the lives of those who were guided by the Holy Spirit throughout life's journey.

God alone knows exactly what we must endure in order to form his character in us.

> It is in our trials that God refines us and removes our impurities. Like refined gold, when we pass through our trials, people will see His perfect reflection in us. (Wendy Blight, *Hidden*

Joy in a Dark Corner: The Transforming Power of God's Story)

I know you may be saying that I have been on a journey all my life. I agree; we all have been on a journey. However, now you will become an active participant in your journey. You will no longer passively sit by and let life happen to you; you will actively engage life by conscientiously becoming the author of your personal life story with the help of the Holy Spirit.

Pearls of Wisdom #3. The Holy Spirit is God's GPS in the life of every believer. He determines our location, our position, and our velocity. He monitors our well-being and our readiness to engage the next phase of our journey. The Holy Spirit is the conduit by which God communicates with us and assists in navigating our journey.

Pearls of Wisdom #4. Beware of signal blockers: distractions such as people, situations, busyness, social media, or other things or platforms that can prevent or distort communication between you and the Holy Spirit.

Chapter 2

THE PROMISE, THE WILDERNESS, AND THE PROMISED LAND

Believe me, my journey has not been a simple journey of progress. There have been many ups and downs, and it is the choices that I made at each of those times that have helped shape what I have achieved.

—Satya Nadella
(retrieved November 10, 2018)

The Holy Spirit acts as a GPS receiver to accurately determine your position and guide you to your next destination. Once the GPS knows your exact location, then it can chart your course detailing all routes possible to your next destination.

This is the role of the Holy Spirit in the life of the believer. He determines your position and charts the best route that will take you to your next destination. If you have ever used a GPS, then you know that when you type in a destination, the first route shown is the fastest route to that destination. It also lets you know how long it will take you to get there dependent on traffic. GPS devices will also show you if there are toll roads, accidents, or bad weather conditions along your journey. The Holy Spirit will reveal to the believer the same information if he or she will allow. He will let you know how costly the journey will be or if there is danger ahead. The Holy Spirit will guide us throughout every step of our journey if we will allow.

> But when He, the Spirit of Truth (the Truth-giving Spirit) comes, He will guide you into all the Truth (the whole, full Truth). For He will not speak His own message [on His own authority]; but He will tell whatever He hears [from the Father He will give the message that has been given to Him], and He will announce *and* declare to you the things that are to come [that will happen in the future]. (John 16:13, Amp)
>
> And Jesus, when he was baptized, went up straightway out of the water: and, lo, the heavens were opened unto him, and he saw the Spirit of God descending like a dove, and lighting upon him: And lo a voice from heaven, saying, This is my beloved Son, in whom I am well pleased. Then was Jesus led up of the Spirit into the wilderness to be tempted of the devil. And when he had fasted forty days and forty nights, he was afterward an hungered. (Matthew 3:16, 17; 4:1, 2, KJV)

As discussed in chapter 1, the Holy Spirit leads or guides us into all truth, i.e., the truth as revealed to him by the Father (our own personal satellite system). The Father provides the information that we need to guide us throughout the entirety of our journey. The Holy Spirit, as the receiver, processes this information and uploads it into our spirit so that we can choose a path to take; albeit, the ability or capacity of the believer to follow the guidance of the Holy Spirit takes growth, maturity, and time. I believe that most people are under the assumption that the Holy Spirit will not lead them into places that appear to be unseemly; however, according to the scripture, the Holy Spirit will lead us into our very own personal "wilderness," just as he did Jesus, in order to have what I believe to be a divine personal encounter with ourselves and with him. We must face the man in the mirror. We must have an intimate relationship with ourselves. We must know our likes, dislikes, weaknesses, and temptations because these may serve as signal blockers throughout our journey. They can thwart our purpose, leaving us incapacitated to accomplish the very thing that we were born to do.

During his wilderness experience, Jesus confronted three aspects of human nature that all of us are bombarded with daily.

> Then was Jesus led up of the Spirit into the wilderness to be tempted of the devil.
>
> And when he had fasted forty days and forty nights, he was afterward an hungered.
>
> And when the tempter came to him, he said, If thou be the Son of God, command that these stones be made bread. But he answered and said, It is written, Man shall not live by bread alone,

but by every word that proceedeth out of the mouth of God. Then the devil taketh him up into the holy city, and setteth him on a pinnacle of the temple, And saith unto him, If thou be the Son of God, cast thyself down: for it is written, He shall give his angels charge concerning thee: and in their hands they shall bear thee up, lest at any time thou dash thy foot against a stone. Jesus said unto him, It is written again, Thou shalt not tempt the Lord thy God. Again, the devil taketh him up into an exceeding high mountain, and sheweth him all the kingdoms of the world, and the glory of them; And saith unto him, All these things will I give thee, if thou wilt fall down and worship me. Then saith Jesus unto him, Get thee hence, Satan: for it is written, Thou shalt worship the Lord thy God, and him only shalt thou serve. Then the devil leaveth him, and, behold, angels came and ministered unto him. (Matthew 4:1–11, KJV)

The Greek term for "tempted" is *peirazo* which means to try or test for the purpose of ascertaining his quantity or what he thinks or how he will behave himself (Strong, 1990). It also describes one who attempts to test someone maliciously or craftily to put to the proof his feelings or judgments regarding some concept, person, or situation. It means to test one's faith, virtue, or character by enticement to sin or to scrutinize, entice, discipline (Strong). Thus, Jesus was tempted in every imaginable way, yet he did not falter. The Holy Spirit not only led him into the wilderness to be tempted, but he gave him the capacity to endure the trial. Trials or adverse conditions are necessary in our journey for they build character and facilitate humility and compassion. The Apostle James said it thusly, "The trying of your faith worketh patience. But let patience have her perfect work, that ye may be perfect and entire, wanting nothing" (James 1:3–4).

The Greek word for "perfect" is *teleios* and may be defined as mature (consummated) from going through the necessary stages to reach the end goal, i.e., developed into a consummating completion by fulfilling the necessary process or spiritual journey (Strong). The Greek word for "entire" is *holokléros* and is defined as complete in *every* part and sound (Strong). Everything we experience throughout our journey has been specifically tailor-made for each of us and is designed to refine, mature, and make us sound in the essence of our being for that place of greatness or that high place that God has called each of us to. When we fail to be properly processed for these high places, then one of two things is possible: either you won't make it to your designated place settling for less than what was intended for your life or when you make it to the high places, jealousy, insecurity, and fear will suffocate you, incapacitating you to sustain your position.

> Trials, temptations, disappointments—all these are helps instead of hindrances, if one uses them rightly. They not only test the fiber of character but strengthen it. Every conquering temptation represents a new fund of moral energy. (James Buckham)

Please don't misconstrue what I am attempting to say. Everyone has experienced some sort of trial or mishap at some point in their life that was the result of a choice or decision. However, regardless of which place you find yourself because of the path chosen, the Holy Spirit can and will use the good, the bad, and the ugly to orchestrate your path to destiny. Remember the children of Israel on the road to the "Promised Land" that God had pledged to give to them from the time of Abraham. Moses led them from a land of bondage—Egypt—into the wilderness. Why? Why was it necessary for the children of Israel to go through the wilderness prior to the Promised Land? Let's take a closer look into the journeyings of the children of Israel. Again, it is not my intention to engage in a textual criticism here but rather to try and describe how the Holy Spirit leads us to and through some of the most difficult places in our lives in our fulfillment of purpose. Before we look at the wilderness experiences of the children of Israel, it is necessary to look at God's promise to the children of Israel as well as his affirmation of them.

The Promise

In Genesis 12:1, God makes several promises to Abraham regarding his posterity.

> Now the LORD had said unto Abram, Get thee out of thy country, and from thy kindred, and from thy father's house, unto a land that I will shew thee: And I will make of thee a great nation, and I will bless thee, and make thy name great; and thou shalt be a blessing: And I will bless them that bless thee, and curse him that curseth thee: and in thee shall all families of the

earth be blessed...And Abram passed through the land unto the place of Sichem, unto the plain of Moreh. And the Canaanite was then in the land. And the LORD appeared unto Abram, and said, Unto thy seed will I give this land: and there builded he an altar unto the LORD, who appeared unto him. (Genesis 12:1–3, 6, 7)

And the LORD said unto Abram, after that Lot was separated from him, Lift up now thine eyes, and look from the place where thou art northward, and southward, and eastward, and westward: For all the land which thou seest, to thee will I give it, and to thy seed forever. (Genesis 13:14, 15)

And when the sun was going down, a deep sleep fell upon Abram; and, lo, an horror of great darkness fell upon him. And he said unto Abram, Know of a surety that thy seed shall be a stranger in a land that is not theirs, and shall serve them; and they shall afflict them four hundred years; And also that nation, whom they shall serve, will I judge: and afterward shall they come out with great substance. And thou shalt go to thy fathers in peace; thou shalt be buried in a good old age. But in the fourth generation they shall come hither again: for the iniquity of the Amorites is not yet full. And it came to pass, that, when the sun went down, and it was dark, behold a smoking furnace, and a burning lamp that passed between those pieces. In the same day the LORD made a covenant with Abram, saying, Unto thy seed have I given this land, from the river of Egypt unto the great river, the river Euphrates: The Kenites, and the Kenizzites, and the Kadmonites, And the Hittites, and the Perizzites, and the Rephaims, And the Amorites, and the Canaanites, and the Girgashites, and the Jebusites. (Genesis15:12–21)

When God called Abram (hereafter referred to as Abraham), he was in the city of Ur located in the province of Babylonia. Ur was considered to be a very advanced city with libraries, schools, and a system of law. God had promised Abraham that he would make his name great and that through his descendants, he would make him a *great nation* and that he would provide for his seed a land that would stretch from the Nile River of Egypt unto the great river Euphrates. However, he also revealed to Abraham that his seed would find themselves under Egyptian rule for specific amount of time.

God made Abraham a promise, and he also forewarned him of the impending captivity of his posterity. God also promised Abraham that a "deliverer" would ultimately come through his lineage and orchestrate their deliverance and freedom. Abraham had a choice: leave that which he was most familiar with, his family, his friends, his land, and his stability, or continue a life of tradition, complacency, and/or contentment. At first glance, it would appear that Abraham was sacrificing a lot for a promise that may have been seen as vague or far reaching. How often have you been given an opportunity of a lifetime that seemed almost too good to be true? How many times have you had to contemplate leaving a "place" of stability that you had become accustomed to? How many of you have had to forsake family and friends to go after a promise that you believed God made to you? Now you have some understanding as to what Abraham may have been feeling when God presented him with this promise. The choice was Abraham's, and no one could make that choice but him. He knew the cost and ramifications of his decision, not only for himself but for his posterity as well. Abraham made the choice to follow after God. God led him every step of the way, and Abraham became a very prosperous man.

Almost 215 years later, Abraham's seed was still under Egyptian rule. A young Israelite, who was reared in the courts of Pharaoh, had been groomed all of life for this one specific reason: to deliver the children of Israel, his heritage, from the rule of Pharaoh. Pharaoh was threatened by the presence of the children of Israel. He was greatly concerned that these people who had transitioned into a great nation would one day arise and afflict his people. Thus, he commanded that all newborn Hebrew boys be cast into the river as soon as they were born.

> And he said unto his people, Behold, the people of the children of Israel are more and mightier than we: Come on, let us deal wisely with them; lest they multiply, and it come to pass, that, when there falleth out any war, they join also unto our enemies, and fight against us, and so get them up out of the land. Therefore, they did set over them taskmasters to afflict them with their burdens. And they built for Pharaoh

treasure cities, Pithom and Raamses. But the more they afflicted them, the more they multiplied and grew. And they were grieved because of the children of Israel. And the Egyptians made the children of Israel to serve with rigour: And they made their lives bitter with hard bondage, in morter, and in brick, and in all manner of service in the field: all their service, wherein they made them serve, was with rigour. And the king of Egypt spake to the Hebrew midwives, of which the name of the one was Shiphrah, and the name of the other Puah: And he said, When ye do the office of a midwife to the Hebrew women, and see them upon the stools; if it be a son, then ye shall kill him: but if it be a daughter, then she shall live. But the midwives feared God and did not as the king of Egypt commanded them, but saved the men children alive. And the king of Egypt called for the midwives, and said unto them, why have ye done this thing, and have saved the men children alive? And the midwives said unto Pharaoh, Because the Hebrew women are not as the Egyptian women; for they are lively and are delivered ere the midwives come in unto them. Therefore, God dealt well with the midwives: and the people multiplied and waxed very mighty. And it came to pass, because the midwives feared God, that he made them houses. And Pharaoh charged all his people, saying, every son that is born ye shall cast into the river, and every daughter ye shall save alive. (Exodus 1:9–22, KJV)

Although born a Hebrew, Moses was well acquainted with the culture, laws, and customs of the Egyptian people. God had groomed him to speak the language of two very diverse cultures. When Pharaoh was convinced to release the children of Israel through a series of convincing manifestations of the power of God (Exodus 7:14–12:23), Moses led them from Rameses to Succoth, through the Red Sea on dry ground, and to the Wilderness of Sin where they spent the majority of their time, roughly around thirty-eight years.

The *Wilderness of Sin* is mentioned in the Bible as being one of the places that the Israelites wandered during their Exodus. The children of Israel spent close to forty years in this wilderness prior to their entrance into the Promised Land. Although they made several stops prior to their entrance, only their time spent in the Wilderness of Sin is highlighted here.

I am only highlighting the wilderness experiences here, though I believe every place the children of Israel journeyed holds significance. I believe that wilderness experiences are designed in part to do two things. First, wilderness experiences are designed to assist the individual to engage or confront their fears, motives, insecurities, doubts, weaknesses, and strengths. In doing so, the individual has a divine encounter with himself or herself as well as with God. Krummacher (1837) stated that a spiritual wilderness means to be deprived of every support, in which the individual might place his confidence, which consequently compels him to fix his hopes solely on the living God, for he never does this as long as he has anything left with which he can commit idolatry, which must therefore be taken from him. This privation of all support is spiritually both of an external and internal nature and sometimes combined.

Secondly, wilderness experiences are designed to facilitate a paradigm shift within the individual. A paradigm is an accepted model or pattern (Kuhn, 1996). A paradigm is a group of theories or ideas that have been shaped by an individual's belief system, upbringing, schooling, and culture. A person's paradigm about how the government should be operated funds their behavior about how much input the government should have in state operations as well as people's lives. A person's paradigm regarding marriage in the traditional sense may fund their support or lack thereof of nontraditional marriages. A paradigm shift occurs when one's existing paradigm is confronted with a paradigm that is contradictory to what they have become accustomed to. In the scientific community, Thomas Kuhn would deem this as a scientific revolution. Scientific revolutions are in part those tradition-shattering complements to tradition-bound activity (Kuhn). In other words, a paradigm shift occurs when some revolutionary event changes your tradition-bound perspective about subjects or systems that you were indoctrinated in and therefore had become accustomed. Your personal *wilderness* experience should align your thinking with God's thinking and prepare you for your place of greatness, which for the children of Israel was their very own Promised Land. There is a Promised Land for all of us, and our ability to navigate our wilderness with the guidance of the Holy Spirit will determine if we make it over to our Promised Land or how well we will handle the successes and challenges that we will face when we get there.

Notice that throughout their journey, the children of Israel complained three times to Moses because of the perils experienced at various times throughout their journey and hence their desire to return to Egypt, the place of bondage. They had become complacent and even comfortable in this place of bondage. Now, let's not judge them to fast as we muse over their murmurings. How many times have you experienced difficulty, fear, insecurity, and inadequacy during your life? How many of you have questioned God and his ability to provide for you? How many times have you questioned God's ability to lead you? How many of you can look back and see how God provided, protected, and led you at some of the most difficult times in life? Now, how many of you can look back and now realize why it was necessary and even beneficial to take the path that you did?

I recall the number of times that I have complained throughout my own personal journey. Although God always provided for me and protected me through some of my most challenging wilderness experiences, as soon as I experienced discomfort or fear from another difficult situation, I whined, cried, and complained as do many of you. In retrospect, most things I have experienced have helped shape the person that I am today. I have learned many lessons from my wilderness experiences. Understand that when you don't learn from your trials or experiences, you are subject to repeat them. It is similar to learning a new concept in school. The knowledge gained and the skill set acquired are needed for the next lesson. If you don't get the prerequisite knowledge or skill set needed, then you will more than likely struggle with the next lesson. Moreover, when individuals attempt to go to college, there are certain prerequisite courses they may need depending upon their major. If these individuals lack these courses, then they will have to take remedial courses.

Wilderness experiences are designed to strengthen you, help you to face your greatest fears, overcome feelings of rejection, and triumph over feelings of insecurity. In other words, wilderness experiences are periods in your life where you have a divine encounter with yourself and God, whereby he shows you the very contents of your heart.

> And thou shalt remember all the way which the LORD thy God led thee these forty years in the wilderness, *to humble thee*, and *to prove thee*, *to know what was in thine heart*, whether thou wouldest keep his commandments, or no.
> And he humbled thee, and suffered thee to hunger, and fed thee with manna, which thou knewest not, neither did thy fathers know; that he might make thee know that man doth not live by bread only, but by every word that proceedeth out of the mouth of the LORD doth man live. (Deuteronomy 8:1, 2)

God told the children of Israel that he led them to and through the wilderness to incite humility, to prove them, and to show them what was in their heart. These were the prerequisite experiences that they needed in Canaan or the Promised Land. Be reminded that no one over the age of twenty, except Joshua and Caleb, made it into Canaan because of their constant murmuring.

> And the LORD spake unto Moses and unto Aaron, saying, How long shall I bear with this

evil congregation, which murmur against me? I
have heard the murmurings of the children of
Israel, which they murmur against me. Say unto
them, As truly as I live, saith the LORD, as ye have
spoken in mine ears, so will I do to you: Your
carcasses shall fall in this wilderness; and all that
were numbered of you, according to your whole
number, from twenty years old and upward
which have murmured against me. Doubtless ye
shall not come into the land, concerning which I
sware to make you dwell therein, save Caleb the
son of Jephunneh, and Joshua the son of Nun.
But your little ones, which ye said should be a
prey, them will I bring in, and they shall know
the land which ye have despised. But as for you,
your carcasses, they shall fall in this wilderness.
(Numbers 14:26–32)

Again, God told Moses that one of the reasons he brought the
children of Israel to the wilderness was to incite humility or humble
them and to prove them so that they would know what was in their
heart. The Hebrew term for "humble" is *anah* (Strong). *Anah* means
to afflict as a discipline, to chasten, or even to debase (Strong) The
Hebrew term for "prove" is *nasah* and means to test or to try (Strong),
and the Hebrew term for "to know" is *yada* (Strong) and means to
bring forth and/or to become acquainted with. I am sure that it is
difficult to imagine that God would permit his people to experience
the difficulties and hardships that they encountered during their wilderness experiences. But if we read further, we discover that God had

a purpose even in this. God knows what we are capable and incapable of no matter what we say or even think. He knows the contents of our heart even though we may not. He knows the path that we must take in order to bring to light those things that can serve to undermine us as we aspire to the *greatness* that he placed on the inside of each one of us. Remember the old adage, "Don't let your aptitude take you where your attitude can't keep you." Your wilderness experience is designed to facilitate a paradigm shift in you. Your personal wilderness experience can be a place of stagnation and death, or it can be your place of empowerment. Remember, everyone that entered the wilderness did not leave the wilderness.

The Exodus author does not expressly suggest that the Holy Spirit was leading the children of Israel but rather used metaphors to describe how God guided them through their wilderness experience. God led the children of Israel by a pillar of cloud by day and a pillar of fire by night. The pillars of cloud and fire are symbolic of the presence of God.

> And the LORD went before them by day in a pillar of a cloud, to lead them the way; and by night in a pillar of fire, to give them light; to go by day and night: He took not away the pillar of the cloud by day, nor the pillar of fire by night, from before the people. (Exodus 13:21–22)

God made provisions for the children of Israel throughout their journey, but they never stopped complaining. They refused to confront their shortcomings and allow God to facilitate a paradigm shift in their way of thinking. They had relied on the Egyptian's system of government, religion, education, and finances for so long that they found it difficult to consistently trust in a monotheistic system where God, himself, provided for his people.

We understand that the pillar of cloud by day and fire by night was simply a foreshadowing of how the Holy Spirit would lead us in the days to come. Thus, God used other conduits to lead his people. It wasn't until Jesus came that we began to see and understand how the Holy Spirit would eventually lead the believer.

When Jesus was baptized by John in the River Jordan (Luke 3:21, 22), it was recorded that the Holy Spirit descended on him in "bodily shape" like a dove when he emerged from the Jordan River.

> Now when all the people were baptized, it came to pass, that Jesus also being baptized, and praying, the heaven was opened, And the Holy Ghost descended in a bodily shape like a dove upon him, and a voice came from heaven, which said, Thou art my beloved Son; in thee I am well pleased. (Luke 3:21, 22)

In the above passage of the scripture, the Holy Spirit is compared to that of a dove. After God affirmed his sonship, Jesus was immediately led into the wilderness by the Holy Spirit to be tempted of the devil in preparation for his earthly ministry and kingdom reign.

> And Jesus being full of the Holy Ghost returned from Jordan, and was led by the Spirit into the wilderness, Being forty days tempted of

the devil. And in those days he did eat nothing: and when they were ended, he afterward hungered. And the devil said unto him, If thou be the Son of God, command this stone that it be made bread. And Jesus answered him, saying, It is written, That man shall not live by bread alone, but by every word of God. And the devil, taking him up into an high mountain, shewed unto him all the kingdoms of the world in a moment of time. And the devil said unto him, All this power will I give thee, and the glory of them: for that is delivered unto me; and to whomsoever I will I give it. If thou therefore wilt worship me, all shall be thine. And Jesus answered and said unto him, Get thee behind me, Satan: for it is written, Thou shalt worship the Lord thy God, and him only shalt thou serve. And he brought him to Jerusalem, and set him on a pinnacle of the temple, and said unto him, If thou be the Son of God, cast thyself down from hence: For it is written, He shall give his angels charge over thee, to keep thee: And in their hands they shall bear thee up, lest at any time thou dash thy foot against a stone. And Jesus answering said unto him, It is said, Thou shalt not tempt the Lord thy God. And when the devil had ended all the temptation, he departed from him for a season. And Jesus returned in the power of the Spirit into Galilee:

and there went out a fame of him through all the region round about. (Luke 4:1–14)

In chapter 1, I described what happened during Jesus's wilderness experience. Now, this is what happened after he returned.

> And Jesus returned in the power of the Spirit into Galilee: and there went out a fame of him through all the region round about... And he came to Nazareth, where he had been brought up: and, as his custom was, he went into the synagogue on the Sabbath day, and stood up for to read. And there was delivered unto him the book of the prophet Esaias. And when he had opened the book, he found the place where it was written, The Spirit of the Lord is upon me, because he hath anointed me to preach the gospel to the poor; he hath sent me to heal the brokenhearted, to preach deliverance to the captives, and recovering of sight to the blind, to set at liberty them that are bruised, To preach the acceptable year of the Lord. (Luke 4:18)

Notice that when Jesus returned from the wilderness, he returned in the *power* of the Spirit. The Greek word for "power" is *dunamis* (Strong, 1990) and can be defined as ability, strength, might, or miraculous power. The term *dunamis* is also used in Acts 1:8:

> But ye shall receive power, after that the
> Holy Ghost is come upon you: and ye shall be
> witnesses unto me both in Jerusalem, and in all
> Judea, and in Samaria, and unto the uttermost
> part of the earth. (Acts 1:8, KJV)

> But you shall receive power (ability, effi-
> ciency, and might) when the Holy Spirit has
> come upon you, and you shall be My witnesses
> in Jerusalem and all Judea and Samaria and to the
> ends (the very bounds) of the earth. (Acts 1:8,
> Amp)

Thus, it is the Holy Spirit who empowers the believer to fulfill purpose. The Greek word for "anointed" is *chrio* which means to smear or rub with oil. Anoint means to consecrate for office or religious service. During biblical times, individuals were anointed with oil to signify God's blessing upon their life.

> Then shalt thou take the anointing oil, and
> pour it upon his head, and anoint him. (Exodus
> 29:7)

> And thou shalt set up the court round
> about, and hang up the hanging at the court gate.
> And thou shalt take the anointing oil, and anoint
> the tabernacle, and all that is therein, and shalt
> hallow it, and all the vessels thereof: and it shall
> be holy. And thou shalt anoint the altar of the
> burnt offering, and all his vessels, and sanctify
> the altar: and it shall be an altar most holy. And

thou shalt anoint the laver and his foot, and sanctify it. And thou shalt bring Aaron and his sons unto the door of the tabernacle of the congregation, and wash them with water. And thou shalt put upon Aaron the holy garments, and anoint him, and sanctify him; that he may minister unto me in the priest's office. And thou shalt bring his sons, and clothe them with coats: And thou shalt anoint them, as thou didst anoint their father, that they may minister unto me in the priest's office: for their anointing shall surely be an everlasting priesthood throughout their generations. (Exodus 40:8–15)

And he arose, and went into the house; and he poured the oil on his head, and said unto him, Thus saith the LORD God of Israel, I have anointed thee king over the people of the LORD, even over Israel. (2 Kings 9:6)

Let thy garments be always white; and let thy head lack no ointment. (Ecclesiastes 9:8)

There are three things apparent after Jesus's wilderness experiences: (1) He returned in the power of the Holy Spirit; (2) he was anointed and set apart for purpose; and (3) he began to operate fully in his purpose. The affirmation of Jesus after his baptism and the wilderness experience precipitated the purpose to which he was to accomplish during his time on earth. Upon Jesus's return from the wilderness, he proclaims:

The Spirit of the Lord is upon me, because he hath anointed me to preach the gospel to the poor; he hath sent me to heal the brokenhearted, to preach deliverance to the captives, and recovering of sight to the blind, to set at liberty them that are bruised, To preach the acceptable year of the Lord. (Luke 4:18)

The Spirit of the Lord [is] upon Me, because He has anointed Me [the Anointed One, the Messiah] to preach the good news (the Gospel) to the poor; He has sent Me to announce release to the captives and recovery of sight to the blind, to send forth as delivered those who are oppressed [who are downtrodden, bruised, crushed, and broken down by calamity], To proclaim the accepted *and* acceptable year of the Lord [the day when salvation and the free favors of God profusely abound]. (Luke 4:18, 19, Amplified Bible)

After the wilderness experience, Jesus proclaimed that the Holy Spirit had anointed him to (1) preach the gospel, (2) to heal the brokenhearted, (3) to preach deliverance to the captives, (4) to recover the sight to the blind, and (5) to pronounce liberty to those who have been imprisoned physically, spiritually, and emotionally. Jesus had a relationship with the Holy Spirit and understood the role of the Holy Spirit in his earthly ministry.

Relationship Between the Believer and the Holy Spirit

It is important to understand the relationship between the believer and the Holy Spirit. However, before I elaborate on the relationship between the believer and the Holy Spirit, I want to provide a brief description of how the relationship between the believer and the Holy Spirit is similar to how we use a GPS receiver.

In order for a GPS receiver to work properly, there must be a direct line of communication between the satellites and the GPS; otherwise, the GPS receiver will not be able to assist the individual in getting to his or her destination at the appointed time. When an individual has determined a destination, he or she must enter the address into the GPS which in turn receives, decodes, and translates radio signals from the satellites so that the individual will know the direction to take. Of course, there are times when we don't have a specific destination in mind but rather a general destination such as dining, shopping, or fuel stops. These destinations are referred to as points of interest on the GPS receiver and are there to provide the individual with a variety of locations specific or suitable to his or her needs or interests. From a more global perspective, these destinations can be likened to the various destinations that believers travel throughout their journey in life as they fulfill their purpose.

Prior to his wilderness experience, Jesus was baptized by John the Baptist. Baptism represented one's submission and obedience to the will of God. Thus, Jesus made a conscious decision to relinquish his will, his gifts, and his talents in submission to God which was a picture for every believer. Once he relinquished the totality of who he was (commonly referred to as the Kenosis of Christ), the Holy

Spirit descended upon him and led him into the wilderness to be tempted. After a time, Jesus returned in the power of the Holy Spirit. Most believers want to be imbued with "power" to preach the word, heal the sick, and preach deliverance to them that are captive without having to go through the wilderness. We want to achieve status and success without this experience. It is not a secret that Jesus was said to have performed his first miracle at the age of twelve; however, it seems that *many* of his miracles occurred after his plight in the wilderness. Again, the Bible records in Luke 4:1 that Jesus was led by the Holy Spirit into the wilderness; however, we read in verse 4 of the same chapter that he returned in the power of the Holy Spirit. There is a clear distinction here. Jesus returned in the power and authority the Holy Spirit.

It is in our wilderness experience that we experience the paradigm shift mentioned earlier in this chapter. All of our beliefs, biases, and traditions are challenged in the wilderness. We have a divine encounter with God and with ourselves. The amount of time that each of us spends in the wilderness is dependent on whether or not we gain the knowledge and skills that we will need for the remainder of our journey. Once we complete this portion of the journey, the Holy Spirit anoints us to accomplish our God-given destiny.

Now let's delve a bit deeper into how using a GPS receiver is realized between the *believer* and the Holy Spirit. In order for a civilian to effectively use the GPS receiver, he or she must understand how it works. One must become familiar with the operating manual and then practice using the GPS receiver. For example, you have been invited to celebrate a friend's job promotion at a new restaurant. You have heard of this venue but have no idea where it is located. You enter the address into your GPS receiver and wait for it to provide you with directions. The GPS not only provides you with step-by-step directions, but it also provides you with alternate routes that you can take as well as the time that it will take to get you there. Most of us rely on a GPS to get us to a specific location. Remember, there are points of interest on the GPS that serve to fit the needs of the individual. One icon that is very important on your GPS is the icon labeled *Home.* If you ever get lost or can't find your destination, you can always press Home, and the GPS will tell how to get back home and you can try again at a later time.

Part of the role of the Holy Spirit is to lead us throughout our journey and help us to traverse life's difficult challenges. This requires us to know him in an intimate way. Now, I must say that a relationship with the Holy Spirit is personal, and he will relate to each of us based on our individual makeup. It is important for you to understand this so that you will not attempt to emulate someone else's relationship with the Holy Spirit in your aspiration to know him. I did this early on in my relationship with him. There are some *great* authors and teachers who have provided awesome insights as to how to establish a relationship with the Holy Spirit to include Benny Hinn, J. G. Packer, and many others. In his book entitled *Good Morning Holy Spirit*, Benny Hinn writes about hours spent in the presence of the Holy Spirit. I tried several times to spend hours in his presence and have yet to be able to do it. Between family, ministry, and work, I am fortunate to spend any quality time in worship. By quality, I mean carving out some time in your day to talk with him about any and everything. I got up every morning and worshipped which consisted of me talking to him and singing songs of adoration with thanksgiving. Some mornings were simply beautiful, and some mornings I simply fell asleep in his presence. When I realized that

God loved my worship and loved that I simply talked to him, I felt so liberated. It is very important to know and understand that in terms of relationship, God deals with each of us on a very personal level. Once you stop emulating or mimicking others' relationship with him, your relationship will begin to thrive. I refuse to allow my relationship with him to be defined by others.

Some people may find that the best time of day to spend with the Holy Spirit is in the early hours of the morning between three and six; however, if you are a doctor who must work in the emergency room during those hours, then is it fair to say that you have missed out on spending quality time with him? Absolutely not! God knows you have to work those hours and completely understands. You must determine what works best for you. Some of my best times spent with the Holy Spirit were on my drive to work when I simply talked to him about some of my deepest fears and concerns or when I questioned him about my situation in life. Most times, I would leave his presence encouraged and ready to take on the world for a few hours, and then I started feeling discouraged again. In these instances, I would simply steal away and talk to him (if time and space permitted). Some days I would spend a couple hours in prayer, and other days it may have been thirty minutes. You will know what works best for you. But know that it is imperative that you spend quality time with him so that you can get the instructions and insights needed for the journey. Furthermore, there are aspirations, ideas, and inventions that you have inside you, and you need the Holy Spirit to give you direction as to what should be done to accomplish these goals or how to make these ideas become a reality.

In the next sections, I want to talk a bit more about these wilderness experiences and how purposeful and necessary they are and how the Holy Spirit will lead you every step of the way if you let him. You can traverse your wilderness experiences blindly or in faith and trust. There are three aspects of the wilderness that you will experience: pre-wilderness, wilderness, and post-wilderness.

Pre-wilderness Experience

Recall the life of David, king of Israel. We first meet David tending his father's sheep in a field near Bethlehem. Samuel was sent by God to the home of Jesse to anoint the next king of Israel.

> And the LORD said unto Samuel, How long wilt thou mourn for Saul, seeing I have rejected him from reigning over Israel? fill thine horn with oil, and go, I will send thee to Jesse the Bethlehemite: for I have provided me a king among his sons. (1 Samuel 16:1)

Jesse's seven sons are brought before the Prophet Samuel to determine who would be the next king of Israel. After careful scrutiny, Samuel inquires as to whether or not Jesse had anymore sons. Jesse tells Samuel that his youngest son is tending to his flocks. David is beckoned from the field so that he could present himself to the prophet. When this ruddy young man with beautiful eyes and a handsome appearance enters the room, God proclaims to Samuel, "Get up. Anoint him, for this is he!"

> And Samuel said unto Jesse, Are here all thy children? And he said, There remaineth yet

> the youngest, and, behold, he keepeth the sheep.
> And Samuel said unto Jesse, Send and fetch
> him: for we will not sit down till he come hither.
> And he sent, and brought him in. Now he was
> ruddy, and withal of a beautiful countenance,
> and goodly to look to. And the LORD said, Arise,
> anoint him: for this is he. (1 Samuel 16:11, 12)

Before David was anointed by Samuel the prophet, he had been tending his father's flock. It has been said that whenever David "brought out his flocks to pasture, he led the young lambs to graze among the fresh, tender young grasses, for they had not yet any teeth. When the young lambs had nibbled the delicate tips, he next took there the oldest sheep and cows, whose teeth were old and weak, that they might eat the middle part of the stalks which were soft enough for them. Last of all, he used to bring to the field the grown sheep and cattle, whose strong teeth could chew the lowest part of the grass nearest to the roots" (Retrieved from http://www.chabad.org/library/article_cdo/aid/2049/jewish/The-Shepherd-who-became-King.htm).

David's compassion for his father's flock was quite evident in the way he cared for them and protected them.

> And David said unto Saul, Thy servant kept
> his father's sheep, and there came a lion, and a
> bear, and took a lamb out of the flock: And I went
> out after him, and smote him, and delivered it
> out of his mouth: and when he arose against me,
> I caught him by his beard, and smote him, and

slew him. Thy servant slew both the lion and the bear. (1 Samuel 17:34–36a)

Unbeknownst to David, he was already being groomed for king. While he was tending his father's flock, David was acquiring the experiences, skill set, and knowledge base that he would need to reign as king of united Israel. David was not just a shepherd; he was a musician and poet as well. David wrote 73 Psalms (Halley, 2007), and his musical virtuosity is what gained him access to the palace.

Saul's servants said to him, Behold, an evil spirit from God torments you. Let our lord now command your servants here before you to find a man who plays skillfully on the lyre; and when the evil spirit from God is upon you, he will play it, and you will be well. Saul told his servants, find me a man who plays well and bring him to me. One of the young men said, I have seen a son of Jesse the Bethlehemite who plays skillfully, a valiant man, a man of war, prudent in speech *and* eloquent, an attractive person; and the Lord is with him. So Saul sent messengers to Jesse and said, Send me David your son, who is with the sheep. And Jesse took a donkey loaded with bread, a skin of wine, and a kid and sent them by David his son to Saul. And David came to Saul and served him. Saul became very fond of him, and he became his armor-bearer. Saul sent to Jesse, saying, Let David remain in my service,

for he pleases me. And when the evil spirit from
God was upon Saul, David took a lyre and played
it; so Saul was refreshed and became well, and the
evil spirit left him. (1 Samuel 16:15–23)

Remember everything we experience prepares us for greatness.
It is important to remain cognizant of this so you can take full advantage of whatever situation you find yourself in life. I am certain that
David had no idea that his former experiences as a young herder
were in preparation for his future reign as a king. Ask yourself this
question: what is God preparing me for? What has God anointed
or consecrated you for that you have completely forgotten about or
relinquished because of life's challenges?

Some suggest that David was ten years old when he was initially
anointed for the kingly office by Samuel while others suggest that
he was fifteen years of age. David was called a youth by both Saul
and Goliath, a term customarily used of someone between twelve
and twenty. Also, he was not in the army, yet which was required of
all able males over the age of twenty. Although it is not clear as to
David's exact age when he was anointed by Samuel, we do know that
he was indeed a youth.

Again, Jesse made seven of his sons to pass
before Samuel. And Samuel said unto Jesse, The
Lord hath not chosen these. And Samuel said
unto Jesse, Are here all thy children? And he said,
there remaineth yet the youngest, and, behold, he
keepeth the sheep. And Samuel said unto Jesse,

Send and fetch him: for we will not sit down till he come hither (1 Samuel 16:10–11)

And Saul said to David, Thou art not able to go against this Philistine to fight with him: for thou art but a youth, and he a man of war from his youth (1 Samuel 17:33)

Regardless of his age, we know several years passed before David assumed office as king of Judah at thirty (2 Samuel 2:4) and eventually king of Israel at age thirty-seven.

So all the elders of Israel came to the king to Hebron; and King David made a league with them in Hebron before the LORD: and they anointed David king over Israel. David was thirty years old when he began to reign, and he reigned forty years. In Hebron he reigned over Judah seven years and six months: and in Jerusalem he reigned thirty and three years over all Israel and Judah. (2 Samuel 5:3–5)

There was roughly a fifteen- to twenty-year time period between the consecration of David as king and his actual reign as the king of Judah and then Israel. Prior to his ascension to the throne, David encountered a number of physical, emotional, and spiritual challenges. I will refer to this period of time in David's life as his wilderness period.

The Wilderness

This desert path contradicts all that you (the Shepherd) promised. I want to go *up* to the High Places (but we are going away from them now). The High Places are postponed but for how long or why is not told. Just that it is to be. OK, I will do it, as a burnt offering of my heart and to be in your will and do whatever pleases You. (Hannah Hurnard, *Hinds Feet on High Places*, p. 82)

One would automatically assume that once David was anointed, he would have taken the position as king with Saul abdicating the throne immediately. That was not the case. More training was needed for such a position. After David was anointed, he was summoned to the palace to relieve the king of a "tormenting depression" by playing his harp. Each time David played his harp, King Saul was refreshed. Saul was so pleased that he requested David stay in the palace and made him his armor-bearer (1 Samuel 16 13–23). Can you imagine your supervisor informing you that you will be the next chief executive officer (CEO) of the company that you work for? Imagine the anticipation, the excitement. Several months have passed, and you still have not formally assumed the role as CEO; however, you have been asked to serve as the current CEO's right hand man or woman which also involves seemingly menial duties. This was the case with David. David never complained and served the king well. The lesson learned was humility. David had to humble himself before the king and serve him with a most agreeable attitude. This was only the beginning of David's wilderness experience.

Soon after David became armor-bearer to the king, a war between the Philistines and Israel began. A Philistine named Goliath challenged the men of Israel to send a man to fight against him. The Israelites were terrified of Goliath. During this time, David had returned to his father's home to tend the sheep. Later, David's father sent him to take food to his three eldest brothers who were a part of the war against the Philistines. When David heard the ranting of Goliath, he went to Saul to request permission to fight the man who dared to defy the army of the living God. Saul, of course, had his reservations because David was but a youth. Nevertheless, the courage demonstrated by David was unparallel to any he had heard or seen. So as the story goes, David defeated Goliath.

> And the Philistine said to David, Come to me, and I will give thy flesh unto the fowls of the air, and to the beasts of the field. Then said David to the Philistine, Thou comest to me with a sword, and with a spear, and with a shield: but I come to thee in the name of the LORD of hosts, the God of the armies of Israel, whom thou hast defied. This day will the LORD deliver thee into mine hand; and I will smite thee, and take thine head from thee; and I will give the carcasses of the host of the Philistines this day unto the fowls of the air, and to the wild beasts of the earth; that all the earth may know that there is a God in Israel. And all this assembly shall know that the

> Lord saveth not with sword and spear: for the
> battle is the Lord's, and he will give you into our
> hands. And it came to pass, when the Philistine
> arose, and came, and drew nigh to meet David,
> that David hastened, and ran toward the army
> to meet the Philistine. And David put his hand
> in his bag, and took thence a stone, and slang it,
> and smote the Philistine in his forehead, that the
> stone sunk into his forehead; and he fell upon his
> face to the earth. (1 Samuel 17:44–49)

David had confidence that the same God that delivered him from the mouth of the lion and the bear would deliver him from Goliath, and so he did. This incited a greater confidence and trust in the Lord, traits that would be needed when he faced more difficult challenges along his journey. As David had witnessed the hand of the Lord in the pasture, he had now witnessed the hand of the Lord on the battlefield.

It would seem that David would have gained the respect and admiration of King Saul, but it was quite the contrary. Saul was quite livid or wroth with David.

> And it came to pass as they came, when
> David was returned from the slaughter of the
> Philistine, that the women came out of all cities
> of Israel, singing and dancing, to meet King Saul,
> with tabrets, with joy, and with instruments of
> music. And the women answered one another as
> they played, and said, Saul hath slain his thou-

sands, and David his ten thousands. And Saul was very wroth, and the saying displeased him; and he said, they have ascribed unto David ten thousands, and to me they have ascribed but thousands: and what can he have more but the kingdom? And Saul eyed David from that day and forward. (1 Samuel 18:6–8)

The Amplified version of the text states that Saul [jealously] eyed David from that day forward (verse 14). Now, imagine that you have accomplished some huge feat and the same vice president, whose position you thought you were supposed to have, now views you as a threat for his/her position and has nothing but disdain for you. How would you handle a situation like this knowing that he or she is sitting in your supposedly vice president's seat? Although David now had been rejected by Saul, the Bible records that David behaved himself wisely in all of his ways (1 Samuel 18:14b). The Hebrew word for "wisely" is *maskil* and describes one who acts with intelligence. Some translations interpret this notion of wisely as being successful. In other words, David understood what was happening and used his intelligence to act accordingly. This infuriated Saul even more. The lesson learned—integrity and judiciousness in the midst of rejection. David learned the importance of integrity and judicious conduct, characteristics necessary for his future reign as king.

Soon after Saul rejected David, he ran for his life for Saul was now determined to kill him. Although David had in fact done nothing wrong but served the king in whatever capacity needed, he was heartbroken to know that Saul desired nothing more than to destroy him.

> David fled from Naioth in Ramah and came
> and said to Jonathan, What have I done? Of what
> am I guilty? What is my sin before your father,
> that he seeks my life? But Saul cast his spear
> at him to smite him, by which Jonathan knew
> that his father had determined to kill David (1
> Samuel 20:1, 33)

On two different occasions, David held the life of Saul in his very hands but chose not to kill him. His rationale: Saul was still God's anointed king, and thus he refused to kill him and prevented his men from doing so as well. It is important to note that the young man who formerly shepherded his father's flock was now leading hundreds of men, women, and children. Again, remember that these experiences are the data needed in the next phase of your journey.

> And the men of David said unto him,
> Behold the day of which the LORD said unto
> thee, Behold, I will deliver thine enemy into
> thine hand, that thou mayest do to him as it shall
> seem good unto thee. Then David arose, and cut
> off the skirt of Saul's robe privily. And it came
> to pass afterward, that David's heart smote him,
> because he had cut off Saul's skirt. And he said
> unto his men, The LORD forbid that I should do
> this thing unto my master, the LORD's anointed,
> to stretch forth mine hand against him, seeing he
> is the anointed of the LORD. So David stayed his
> servants with these words, and suffered them not

to rise against Saul. But Saul rose up out of the
cave, and went on his way. (1 Samuel 24:4–7)

A characteristic feature of David's was that he frequently sought
the Lord's counsel and direction. Whenever David faced a trial, especially with his enemies, he always asked of the Lord of his will. And
each time he asked, the Lord graciously gave him a clear and definite
answer. David enquired of the Lord nine times, and each time, the
Lord gave him the counsel and direction he needed. This demonstrated tremendous reliance on the Lord for guidance. It also showed
the relationship between David and God.

Then they told David, saying, Behold, the
Philistines fight against Keilah, and they rob
the threshing floors. Therefore David enquired
of the Lord, saying, Shall I go and smite these
Philistines? And the Lord said unto David, Go,
and smite the Philistines, and save Keilah. And
David's men said unto him, Behold, we be afraid
here in Judah: how much more then if we come
to Keilah against the armies of the Philistines?
Then David enquired of the Lord yet again. And
the Lord answered him and said, Arise, go down
to Keilah; for I will deliver the Philistines into
thine hand. (1 Samuel 23:1–4)

And David enquired at the Lord, saying,
Shall I pursue after this troop? shall I overtake
them? And he answered him, Pursue: for thou
shalt surely overtake them, and without fail

recover all. So David went, he and the six hundred men that were with him, and came to the
brook Besor, where those that were left behind
stayed. (1 Samuel 30:8–9)

And it came to pass after this, that David
enquired of the LORD, saying, Shall I go up into
any of the cities of Judah? And the LORD said unto
him, Go up. And David said, Whither shall I go
up? And he said, Unto Hebron. (2 Samuel 2:1)

David faced much opposition during his wilderness experiences.
The above examples were to demonstrate that most of us have found
ourselves at some point in our lives in our own personal wilderness
facing some of the same challenges that David had faced. Throughout
his wilderness experiences, David gained a lot of insight, understanding, patience, compassion, and gumption needed for his future reign
as king. David desperately asked of the Lord at various phases during
his journey, and God led him each step of the way. David learned to
trust and rely on God even more. He confronted and overcame many
obstacles, fear, doubt, despair, rejection, loneliness, and more, and
yet he never left God.

Post-wilderness: Exaltation

There is absolutely no experience, however
terrible, or heartbreaking, or unjust, or cruel,
or evil, which you can meet in the course of
your earthly life, that can harm you if you but
let Me teach you how to accept it with joy; and

to react to it triumphantly as I did myself, with love and forgiveness and with willingness to bear the results of wrong done by others. Every trial, every test, every difficulty and seemingly wrong experience through which you may have to pass, is only another opportunity granted to you of conquering an evil thing and bringing out of it something to the lasting praise and glory of God. (Hurnard, *Mountain of Spices*)

David is now on the precipice of reigning as king of Judah. After the death of Saul, David thought the time had come for him to emerge from exile and assume the helm as the leader of his people. He asked of the Lord once more to determine if the time had come for him to go up to Judah and take the helm of his kingdom.

And it came to pass after this, that David enquired of the LORD, saying, Shall I go up into any of the cities of Judah? And the LORD said unto him, Go up. And David said, Whither shall I go up? And he said, Unto Hebron. (1 Samuel 2:1)

David left Ziklag and proceeded to the ancient city of Hebron in Judah. There, the people of Judah gathered and anointed him king. In the prime and vigor of his life, wise in council, prompt in action, God-fearing, and earnest, David seemed to all men best fitted to be king in those troubled times. He was the warrior king, the poet, and, at times, the priest. At the appointed time, God determined when he was ready to assume the responsibility of king. David started as a shepherd boy tending his father's flock, and now it was time for David to become king of a nation. He first was anointed king of Judah and seven years later king of Israel. David's ascension to the throne was gradual. In each phase of his journey, he learned to a greater degree to trust God. He did not make a move unless he first inquired of the Lord.

When Samuel anointed David, the Spirit of the Lord came upon him from that day forward. The Message Bible records:

> Samuel took his flask of oil and anointed him, with his brothers standing around watching. The Spirit of GOD entered David like a rush of wind, God vitally empowering him for the rest of his life. (1 Samuel 16:13)

The Holy Spirit imbued David with the strength that he would need with what lie ahead. It was the Holy Spirit who enabled David to withstand his wilderness experience while gaining the knowledge and skills that he would need as the future king of united Israel. As king, David would go through many other challenges that would threaten his very position as king, but because these challenges were not completely unfamiliar to him, he knew what his proper response should be. He maintained an attitude of humility and a heart of compassion and forgiveness.

> When there is a mist over the High Mountains where you are going (and you can't see them) you may think they are not real (at times) but then the mist will part for a few moments

some days and frame the truth. You have seen reality, the mist is the illusion. Whatever happens I mean to bring you up there exactly as I promised. (Hannah Hurnard, *Hinds Feet on High Places*, p. 189)

What have you learned from your wilderness experience that has prepared you for your position of greatness? If you did not glean what you needed to in the wilderness, then, like the children of Israel, you are most likely to spend more time in the wilderness than originally intended. You must learn to trust the inner voice of the Holy Spirit. People will say you can't do that when God says that you can. Your family will tell you that you can't accomplish that when God says that you can.

When you have acquired everything needed during your wilderness experience, then you are ready for your Promised Land. You are now on the precipice of greatness, that place between the Wilderness and the Promised Land.

Pearls of Wisdom #5. Don't rush to get to your "Promised Land." You want to be sure that you acquire the requisite knowledge and skills needed for each phase leading up to your "Promised Land."

Pearls of Wisdom #6. Remember, David faced many obstacles throughout his journey. He dealt with his own personal fears, insecurities, and disappointments, all of which prepared him for his future role as king. Let your wilderness prepare you for the assignment or career of a lifetime.

Pearls of Wisdom #7. Wilderness experiences are designed to facilitate a paradigm shift within the individual. All of our beliefs, biases, and traditions are challenged in the wilderness in order to shift our thinking so that we can align ourselves with God's thinking about us. You are great and are called to do great things!

Chapter 3

ON THE PRECIPICE OF GREATNESS

*"I can't go down there," panted Much Afraid,
sick with shock and fear. "He can never mean
there—never." "He called me up to the High
Places, and that Place is an absolute contradiction
of all of this: He promised." "Shepherd," she
said despairingly, "I can't understand this. The
guides you gave me say that we must go down
there into that desert, turning right away from
the High Places altogether. You don't mean that,
do you? You can't contradict yourself. Tell them
we are not to go there and show us another way.
Make a way for us, Shepherd, as you promised."
He looked at her and answered very gently, "That
is the path, Much Afraid, and you are to go down
there. "Oh no," she cried, "You can't mean it. You
said if I would trust you, you would bring me to
the High Places, and that path leads right away
from them. It contradicts all that you promised."*

"No," said the Shepherd, "it is not contradiction,
only postponement for the best to become possible."
—Hurnard,
Hinds' Feet on High Places (p. 108)

*H*inds' Feet on High Places by Hannah Hurnard is an allegorical novel that traces the steps of the main character, Much Afraid, from a frightened, deformed, lost soul to a beautiful and joyful being. Throughout the story, Much Afraid faces countless and almost impossible obstacles on her journey. By overcoming these difficulties, she takes on a new name, Grace and Glory, and is able to see the world from a fresh new perspective.

Before ascending to the High Places, she is lead through the Furnace of Egypt, the Forests of Danger and Tribulation, the Sea of Loneliness, the Precipice Injury, the Valley of Loss, and the Grave on the Mountains. During her passage through these places, her biggest enemies, Resentment, Bitterness, Self-Pity, Pride, and Fear, taunt in ways not difficult to imagine. Much Afraid initially calls on the Shepherd to defeat these enemies but, eventually, is able to overcome them.

I decided to start this chapter with an excerpt from Hurnard's book because it is a familiar place that many of us find ourselves in some point during our journey. Our journey to the higher places or to that place of greatness seems to almost at once descend into what appears to be an abyss. We start out on our journey to greatness and find that our biggest enemies are not simply our friends, family, and significant others but rather those enemies that are lurking in the very recesses of our mind.

I gave my life to Christ at a young age. I recall reading the big white Bible that was on our living room table. Although I could not understand most of what I read, I remember being intrigued with the personage of God. From that time forward, I wanted to live for him no matter what; at least that was my mind-set at the time. I had no idea what it meant to follow the leading of the Holy Spirit. I didn't even know who he was. I later realized that when I committed my life to God, the Holy Spirit was gently guiding me all along.

I am the eldest of three children raised by a single mother. My mother is an extraordinary woman, and I applaud her for raising three children during the time of integration and in the face of adversity and opposition. I remember going to the dentist around the age of seven, and although this was not my first visit to the dentist office, it was my first encounter with racism. While I sat in the room waiting for the doctor to come in, the nurse came in to prep me for his arrival. She placed a napkin around my neck and made sure that I was OK. She then asked me what I wanted to be when I grow up, and I replied, "A doctor."

She then said, "Don't you want to be a maid?"

I said "No."

She asked again, "Don't you want to be a maid?"

Again I replied "No."

This encounter may seem to be minute to some, but the seed of insecurity (one of many) was planted. I often wondered if I was good enough or smart enough to become a doctor. Although I knew nothing of the Holy Spirit's leading, I realize that he was gently guiding me through my life's journey.

As a child, I had low self-esteem. When I started going through puberty, I experienced hair loss and a severe case of acne. I did not like my skin color nor my body type, things most teenagers face. All of the pretty girls seemed to have lighter complexions and long hair. Once, I was hanging out with a group of girls, and we were discussing college sororities. When asked what sorority I wanted to join, I proudly gave the name of the sorority, and one girl exclaimed, "They don't allow 'dark-skinned' girls in that sorority." The seed of doubt, insecurity, and low self-esteem was being firmly established. Although these seeds may seem very minute, the outcome of such seeds can permeate every area of your life.

When I went to college, I majored in biology with hopes of becoming a doctor. It was challenging to say the least. My grades were subpar. I was not focused and was certainly not ready to embark upon a career in medicine; at least this is what I told myself. I talked myself out of a career in medicine. Instead, I decided to get my master's degree in biology with a focus in education. Soon after I graduated, I began my teaching career. I never thought I would become a teacher, but that is where my journey led me. Unbeknownst to me, the Holy Spirit was guiding me. Teaching helped me to acquire a specific skill set needed for my life's purpose. These skills included speaking, organizing content, and writing. During this time, I grew in my relationship with the Holy Spirit. I studied the Bible more, and my prayer life increased. The more I got to know him through his Word and through life experiences, I found myself with a desire to know God more. This evolved over time. I began to ask for his guidance in every area of my life. It was a hit or miss. Sometimes, I got it right, and sometimes, I did not. I realized that God uses the good, the bad, and the ugly to build character, his character, in you.

I taught at an inner-city high school for several years. I started the First Priority Christian Club at my school, and many students took part in this endeavor. It was an enriching and wonderful experience. Many of my former students are doing quite well which is great since the community where many students lived was riddled with violence and drugs. After several years of teaching at the secondary level, I knew that it was time for a change. I prayed for guidance concerning my next career step. I can't say that I waited for an answer. I started applying for jobs at local community colleges. I was interviewed and was politely rejected. After several rejection letters, I was devastated. I thought I was going to cry myself into a coma. I was forced to wait on the Holy Spirit to lead me along the path that he had chosen for me. I ended up going back to school to pursue an educational specialist degree (Ed.S.) in biology education. Upon completion of my Ed.S., I applied for a doctoral program, but as I stated earlier, I was not accepted. I taught for a few more years at the secondary level. I worked hard to improve my craft and ensure that my students were getting a good education. It was difficult, and I felt like I was stuck. I was ready to move on to the next assignment; I had outgrown this position. During those years, I spent time with the Holy Spirit, praying and studying the Bible. It would be seven years later that I would reapply for the doctoral program; however, the circumstances would be different. I called to enquire about the program and was told that I needed to talk with the individual who was the head of the department. This was not the case the first time I had applied. I set up an appointment to talk with him. After I was accepted into the program, the same gentleman became my advisor.

As I mentioned earlier in the book, I was later offered a graduate research assistant's position. The position would require me to quit my job and travel from time to time. Although this would be a big salary cut, the opportunity was great, and it would allow me to be home more. It was all about timing. If I had been accepted into the program a few years earlier, this opportunity would not have existed.

Recall earlier that I stated that my advisor explained to me all of the tasks that I would have to do during my tenure as a doctoral student. Some of these tasks included presentations at local and national conferences, data collection and analyses using statistical procedures and software, publications, comprehensive examinations, and writing a dissertation. I was so overwhelmed, but if it would take me out of the classroom until I could figure what I was going to do next, then so be it. I did not think that I had what it took to complete such a rigorous program. I did not think that I was a good writer since at different times in my life I was told that I could not write. One of my tutors in graduate school told me that she could not believe that I had made it this far in education with my writing skills. Thus, I did not think that I would do well with writing or research. My initial thoughts were that I would complete all of my coursework and then drop out of the program.

As a graduate research assistant, I had to travel to different states with a team of people to collect data in the form of observations, interviews, surveys etc. I learned to input data into Microsoft Excel and the Statistical Package for the Social Sciences (SPSS). I also learned how to conduct basic data analysis. It took some time, but I learned how to do it. By the time I had completed all of my course work, I had become comfortable in data collection and analysis, and my writing was improving. I also had done some national presentations. The Holy Spirit was orchestrating my steps all along. He knew the perfect timing as to when I should start the doctoral program. He knew the opportunities that lay ahead. He knew that I would need such an opportunity to train and provide me with the knowledge and skills that I would need in order to complete this program. He knew that this opportunity would build my confidence.

I completed the program and received my doctor of philosophy degree (PhD) eight years ago. When I completed my program, I thought that now I can start making what I considered to be "good" money and enjoy life. Prior to graduation I started applying for faculty positions, and once again, the rejection letters started. I wasn't as taken aback as I had been those many years before. I knew God was preparing a position for me. My advisor called me and told me about a post-doctoral (post doc) research position that he wanted me to consider after graduation. I had no other options, so unless something else came along, then I would be working as a post doc. I graduated in December and started the post doc position in January, making less money than I made as a high school teacher. I could not believe it. I thought I would be doing better financially than when I was as a teacher, but financially I was not.

Several months after graduation, I found myself at one of the lowest points of my life. I was facing divorce. I am not going to highlight what the problems were, that is not the point of this book, but rather the choice that I made to pursue a divorce. This was by far the most difficult decision of my life. I faced much opposition. But the greatest opposition was internal. My life was crumbling before me, but I knew I had to make a decision. We separated, and I went to live with my mother for a little over a year. Throughout this entire ordeal, I was praying and seeking guidance from the Holy Spirit daily. God did not tell me to divorce; I made the choice. I left a beautiful home and a wonderful community. When we went to live with my mom, my sister and her family of seven were living there as well. My mother had a three-bedroom home. My daughter and I who once enjoyed the pleasures of a four-bedroom home now shared a room and a full-sized bed. I cried every day. What happened? Did I really do the right thing? My life at this point was spiraling out of control. I had a PhD and could not afford to move into a home of my own. God takes the good, the bad, and the ugly to cultivate character in his children. During this time, I worshipped and prayed. I continued to go to church because it was a refuge for me. It was difficult for my daughter. Sometimes, we cried together. I kept her encouraged by telling her that God was going to take good care of us and that our best days lay ahead no matter how dismal it appeared to be.

I continued to apply for faculty positions with no success. I am a firm believer that whatever God has ordained for you regardless of the opposition, you will get it unless you choose to forfeit it by not continuing your journey. My advisor, who now is my supervisor, called me and told me about a part-time position that they needed filled at the beginning of the next semester. I had no other options, so I accepted. This paid less than the post doc position. I didn't understand what was happening. Did I do something wrong? I needed to make more money so that I could move out of my mother's house. Shortly after my supervisor offered me this temporary position, he called me with another opportunity to work as a consultant under another multimillion-dollar grant. This position involved me doing data collection and analyses in classrooms throughout the state. The same skills that I acquired during my doctoral program were needed for this new position. This coupled with my part-time position paid me well. I would be making enough money so that I could move into a place of my own. I was excited and ready to move.

I began putting in applications for rental homes and was told that I did not make enough money. I began to feel discouraged. I had been applying for rental homes in specific parts of the city. The last townhome that I applied for was it, or so I had thought. The gentleman and his wife were former graduates of the university that I completed my doctorate so surely, so surely, they would favor me, especially since I made it my business to tell them I was a former alumnus. This was the first place that I actually got the opportunity to visit because everyone else turned me down. Every place that the sole of my feet treads is mine (Joshua 1:3). I had the faith but was turned down once again. I told God that I was not going to apply for another property. That lasted for only a few days. As I was meditating one morning, I thought that I would look in an area that I had no intention of moving to. I was perusing the area online and found what seemed to be a nice property. I called the landlord, and he told me that I had to be prequalified for the property. My income had not yet begun to come in from my consulting assignment, but I submitted the application anyway; I had nothing to lose. My daughter and I went to view the community and the property. The property was much nicer than any of the other properties we had seen. We immediately loved it. The following day, I called the landlord and told him that I was interested in the house. I completed the remainder of the application and was approved for the townhome within thirty-six hours.

I was ready to begin my new life. I was scared and nervous about my future. I really had to spend time meditating and musing over God's Word to receive instruction for the next steps. I was alone and all I had was my relationship with the Holy Spirit to get me through. Don't get me wrong. I had friends, my church family, and my family praying for me, but it was always about me and the Holy Spirit. Many nights I cried myself to sleep. Honestly, there were times

when I had no idea as to what I should be doing and more importantly whether or not I was on the right path for my life. Had I made
a mistake? Did I take a wrong turn somewhere? Had I missed God?
Although I was teaching and consulting, I felt as though I needed
something more stable. I was teaching at the university through a
grant that would soon come to an end. Although I was fine at the
moment, I was concerned about the future. It was difficult to enjoy
the "now." I realize that I really didn't trust God. In those times when
I was unsure of which direction to take, I patiently waited until I had
some sense of guidance (this required much patience on my part).
I wish I could tell you that I had a detailed conceptual map that
outlined my career path, but I did not. Some people are really good
at mapping out their careers and coming up with a strategic plan as
to how to get their desired job. Unfortunately, that was not the case
with me. It was necessary for me to go the route I did because I am a
better person for it today.

I continued to apply for faculty positions, and to my chagrin—
nothing. Summer was approaching, and my options were few. I did
not teach or consult during the summer months because there were
no opportunities. Honestly, I did not want to be a professor, so my
external actions conflicted with my heart. My supervisor provided
me with a few opportunities that kept some money coming in. Had
I not saved, I would have been in dire straits. My savings were slowly
becoming depleted. Surely, I wouldn't deplete my savings just to live?
Surely [by faith] I would have another source of income by August;
at least that is what I told myself over and over again. August came
and nothing. The consulting position was "hanging in the balance"
because of bureaucratic red tape. I still had the faculty position at
the university, but I would not receive a full check until the end of

September, and that still would not be enough to cover my living expenses.

September came, and I still had no options. No one knew but a select number of people. As far as the world was concerned, I was doing quite well. But those closest to me knew that at times I brought home $900 a month with outgoing expenditures of $4000. These faithful few were true friends. They not only encouraged me but rebuked me when I was in error in my thinking. When I was at my lowest, one friend brought me a CD entitled *I Hope You Dance* by Mark D. Sanders and Tia Sillers that encouraged me to live life to the fullest in spite of the difficulties and uncertainties that I was facing. Although money was strained, somehow, I was making it, and I was living. I took one day at a time. Did I still cry? Yes. But I kept dancing in the midst of tears. I love jazz. A friend's husband, who plays in various bands and with various recording artists throughout the country, told me that occasionally he plays at a local venue, Jazz and Conversations. He invited me to attend as a guest, and I did not have to pay the entrance cost. I was so very appreciative for what I called "special gifts" that God would give me to let me know that everything was going to be okay. October came and still nothing; however, I knew something was on the horizon. A good friend of mine told me about a consulting opportunity with a company that she had done some work for. At the time, the company needed someone with a background in science. I enquired about the position and submitted my resume. They extended an offer, and I accepted. Both the new consulting position and the faculty position combined paid well. By November, I could pay all of my bills and have money to save. Although my money situation was turning around, I continued to apply for faculty positions. I wanted something that provided consistent income but that would allow me the freedom to do consulting or work on other projects. Things were indeed turning around, but more importantly, I had changed, changed for the better. The once insecure, low self-esteem, and always living life superficially individual was now more confident and had positive self-worth about her capabilities and her beauty inside and out. I was living a more purposeful life and enjoying it. I took one day at a time. I was still a "masterpiece" in the making, but I am finally learning to "dance."

I hope you never fear those
mountains in the distance,
Never settle for the path of least resistance
Livin' might mean takin' chances
but they're worth takin',
Lovin' might be a mistake but it's worth makin',
Don't let some hell-bent heart leave you bitter,
When you come close to sellin' out reconsider,
Give the heavens above more
than just a passing glance,
And when you get the choice
to sit it out or dance.

I hope you dance...I hope you dance.
I hope you dance...I hope you dance.
(Time is a wheel in constant motion
always rolling us along,
Tell me who wants to look back on their years
and wonder where those years have gone.)

I hope you still feel small when
you stand beside the ocean,
Whenever one door closes, I
hope one more opens,
Promise me that you'll give
faith a fighting chance,
And when you get the choice
to sit it out or dance.
Dance…I hope you dance.
—"I Hope You Dance"
(Lee Ann Womack)

If you have dealt with insecurities or lacked the confidence or boldness to live your life to the fullest, then I am sure that this song permeated every fiber of your being. Everything that I went through has shaped me into who I am today. Every disappointment, every failure and success helped to mold me into the person that I am today and that I am becoming. Feelings of rejection, betrayal, and abandonment (some of these feelings were self-imposed) made me stronger. I realized that God will use the good, the bad, and the ugly to create a beautiful being. While I gave my life to Christ at a young age, I did not fully commit my life to him until my early twenties. As I look back over my life, I am cognizant that God, through the Holy Spirit, was orchestrating my steps all along.

My mother and father divorced when I was around six years old. I was heartbroken and withdrawn. My sister and I spent the weekends with my dad. I often wondered how my life would have been different had my parents not divorced or if I had gone to live with him. As I stated earlier, it was difficult for my mom raising three children alone. We struggled, but we also had a strong support system which I know contributed to who I am today. My dad and I have a great relationship. He married a wonderful woman, and they have been together for over thirty years. He apologized for not being in our lives more, but I believe there was purpose in that. My dad said that he learned about the true essence of family from my stepmother. You see, he went through what he did to become the wonderful man he is today.

Deepak Chopra, one of the nation's leading advocates of alternative medicine and spirituality, said that he had received a fellowship with one of the country's leading endocrinologist in his early twenties. He stated that he was unhappy with his work and that his supervisor was overbearing.

> My discontent came to a head during a routine staff meeting. My supervisor quizzed me on a technical detail in front of the group: "How many milligrams of iodine did Milne and Greer inject into the rats in their 1959 paper?" This referred to some seminal experimental work, but I answered offhandedly, because he didn't really want the information, only to put me on the spot.
>
> "Maybe two-point-one milligrams. I'll look it up."
>
> "This is something you should have in your head," he barked, irritated. Everyone in the room grew quiet.

I got up, walked over to him, and dumped a bulky file of papers on him. "Now you have it in your head," I said, and walked out.

I was agitated. I walked out to the parking lots and fumbling to start my beat-up Volkswagen Beetle, the signature vehicle of struggling young professionals.

My supervisor followed me fuming, screaming at me, "Your career is ruined."

He leaned in, speaking with studied control to disguise his anger. "Don't," he warned. "You're throwing away your whole career. I can make that happen."

Which was quite true. The word would go out, and with his disapproval, I had no future in endocrinology. But in my mind, I wasn't walking away from a career. I was standing up to someone who had tried to humiliate me in front of the group. My impulsive rebellion was instinctive and yet very unlike me.

I managed to start my Beetle Volkswagen and left him standing there in the hospital.

Word did go out, and I faced the prospect of having no job except for any moonlighting work that might come my way, the lowest paying drudgery in Boston medicine. Pain would follow. I knew this less than five minutes down the road. It made me stop off at a bar before going home to break the devastating news to my wife Rita.

In religion there's an old saw: No one is more dangerous to the faith than an apostate. Boston medicine was the true faith. I had no intention of renouncing it. If you had questioned me the day before I dumped a file on an eminent doctor's head, I would have sworn allegiance. Frankly, I had no reason to change sides, not rationally. You don't walk away from a church when there is no other church to go to. But the only way to see if there are demons lurking outside the circle is to crawl over the boundary that protects you. This was the real start of a revelatory life. I can't take credit for any of the revelations, but a hidden force inside me was invisibly preparing the way.

Yet, I did change sides and soon started "moonlighting" in an emergency room where I started to observe not only the physical trauma of my patients, but their mental anguish. I started to write about their experiences and that started my career in integrative medicine and as a writer. (Chopra, 2013)

My point for inserting this piece into the text was to demonstrate that even though what appeared to be an impulsive decision at the time, it was that decision that promulgated Dr. Chopra into the world to also become a prominent author and speaker.

Throughout my journey, I have come to realize that the Holy Spirit has been cleaning up the mess I had made along the way. I have gained invaluable wisdom and insight throughout this journey that

I will use as the Holy Spirit and I continue to navigate the maze of life. I have learned to trust him more. I have learned to acknowledge him in *everything* I do now. I have learned patience. I have learned the importance of timing. I have learned the importance of being cognizant of everything that takes place in my sphere of living. In other words, I try to be aware of everything that takes place in and around my life as well as that which affects my life locally, nationally, and globally.

Deepak Chopra and Rudolph E. Tanzi stated that "the outcome of your life depends on how you deal with its darkest moments. Will they be turning points or setbacks?" God has indeed given the Holy Spirit to assist us in every facet of our lives. We must take advantage of this special gift that he has given us in the Holy Spirit. Learning to follow his leading takes time. It is a process, and I would dare to even say that it comes through a process of trial and error. It is similar to the relationship between a husband and wife or significant other. You meet and fall in love. However, it could take years to learn what makes your partner behave or think in a particular way. It may take many strong disagreements, successes, and failure before you find that place of marital bliss where the "two become one." Relationships take time. It is no different than our relationship with the Holy Spirit. You probably won't follow someone you don't know because you really don't trust them. How did you come to trust your mother and father? How did you come to trust your spouse? They had to prove themselves several times over before this became realized. Once you established trust, then you knew that person had your best interests in mind. It was a process that gradually grew over time.

I realized that I did not completely trust the Holy Spirit to lead me. I did not trust him completely when I was working for below minimum wage when I completed my doctoral program. I did not trust him completely when I was confined to one room in my mother's home for over a year. In retrospect, I can see the Holy Spirit at work not necessarily in the situation but rather in me. I was a *masterpiece* in the making. Consider the transformation of a caterpillar into a butterfly. Before the emergence of this beautiful creature, it must first go through four stages of development: the egg, the caterpillar (feeding stage), the chrysalis or cocoon (transition stage), and, finally, the butterfly (reproductive stage).

Now I am sure you are wondering what this has to do with following the leading of the Holy Spirit. The butterfly has an "internal clock" that lets it know when it is time to transition into each stage of its life cycle. The Holy Spirit is our internal clock that lets us know when it is time to transition to the next phase or stage of our life. During our feeding/growing phase, we are placed in a variety of contexts specific to our life's purpose. We learn from everything that is within our context of living. There is knowledge and wisdom to be gained and skills to be learned. We take everything and use it as building blocks for our next phase of development. When we enter into that holding place where we are transitioning to that place of greatness, we go through a number of changes. Change is not easy especially for those who do not like change. Everything that is learned during the caterpillar phase and all that we allowed to nourish us will determine how, when, and if we transition into this last stage. We will need our strength, energy, and stored nutrition to assist us in this transformative endeavor. Once the transformative process is complete, you are ready to emerge into the masterpiece that God has created you to be and to fulfill your purpose. Thus, it takes commitment, sacrifice, and a willing heart to accomplish this. Now you are ready to follow him to greater heights still, for it was during those strenuous phases of life that you have come to know him. If you are just beginning your journey, then sit back and enjoy the ride!

We delight in the beauty of the butterfly, but rarely admit the changes it has gone through to achieve that beauty. (Maya Angelou)

Pearls of Wisdom #8. Yes, you have been on a journey since you were born! The idea is to begin a more purposeful journey with the guidance of the Holy Spirit. Allow him to lead you through each phase of your journey as you transition from one phase to the next. Trust me, you will need the requisite knowledge, skills, and experiences for each new phase of your journey.

Chapter 4

TIDBITS FOR THE JOURNEY

The secret of living a life of excellence is merely a
matter of thinking thoughts of excellence. Really,
it's a matter of programming our minds with
the kind of information that will set us free.

—Charles R. Swindoll

At the beginning of chapter 3, I started with a quote from *Hinds Feet on High Places*. At the beginning of the character's journey, she was invited to the *High Places* by the Good Shepherd. We all have an invitation to the High Places. It is our choice as to how high we want to go. There will be difficult places in our journey. The character in Hurnard's book traveled to several places during her ascent to the High Places. Some of these include the following:

1) The Desert
2) The Shores of Loneliness
3) The Forests of Danger and Tribulation
4) The Valley of Loss

There are sacrifices that we make as we ascend to our High Place. It is not always easy, nor does it always feel good. But as they say, nothing in life worth having is easy. You may find yourself in the desert or in situations that appear to be hostile or barren, making it difficult to thrive. You may find yourself in a lonely place where it make you feel like no one else can understand what you are going through, or you may be in a place where there is suffering, distress, pain, unhappiness, agony, heartache, sorrow, anguish, or misery, and you don't know what to do or where to turn. All of these experiences can be very frustrating, but remember, all of these experiences and emotions are designed to make you a masterpiece.

Each time the main character in Hurnard's book overcame her personal fears, inadequacies, rejection, or disappointment, she made some type of memoriam in honor of the Great Shepherd. Each place of triumph incited her to trust him more. We all have fears that we must face. We all have dealt with some form of rejection and experienced disappointment. Many of us have felt inadequate when it came to accomplishing some goal or completing a task.

I have experienced all of these along my journey; however, the greatest challenge I faced was simply knowing who I was and knowing my purpose. This understanding of self was not defined by man but rather by God the more time I spent in his presence and through countless life experiences. With every challenge and uncertainty, I learned more about myself and source of some of my emotions.

I have found that it is not enough to be aware of such feelings, but, rather, stepping back and finding the source of such feelings is essential. In their book, *Super Brain*, Chopra and Tanzi (2012) suggest that awareness of certain feelings is only the beginning of bringing certain emotions or feelings into balance, but it is what they deem as "self-awareness" that makes us unique.

> When you are aware you could be any-
> body, but when you are self-aware, you become
> unique. I am feeling X turns into what do I think
> about X? Where is it taking me? What does it
> mean? Someone who is angry can stop there,
> with almost no self-awareness. An irritable boss
> who chews out his subordinates year after year
> is certainly aware that he gets angry. But with-
> out self-awareness, he won't see what he is doing
> to himself and to others. He might come home
> one day and be flabbergasted that his wife has
> walked out. Once self-awareness dawns in you,
> the questions you can ask about yourself, about
> how you think and feel, have no limit. Self-aware
> questions are the keys that make consciousness
> expand, and when that happens, the possibilities
> are infinite. (p. 88)

According to Chopra and Tanzi, there is a distinct difference between awareness and self-awareness. They suggest that when "you are aware, you pay close attention to the stream of input. You select, decide, sort, and process making choices about what to accept and what to reject. However, when you self-aware, you loop [or reflect] back on what you are doing, asking how is this for me?" (p. 85). Every individual has the capacity to operate this notion of self-aware-ness; this is not difficult to conceive. Reflecting on behaviors, emotions, or actions means asking those difficult questions that have the capacity to challenge the very core of your being.

Dr. Beau Lotto, neuroscientist and founder of Lottolab, during his Ted Talk on Optical Illusions, stated that the creation of all new perceptions begins in the same way, with a single question: "Why?" "Why" is, in that sense, the most dangerous word in history because as soon as you ask that question, you open up the possibility of change. So asking "why" may be the hardest thing for people to do" (Lotto, 2009).

Remember, at the outset of this book, I said that you should consider yourselves as data collectors throughout your journey collecting data that may be used to modify or improve future actions or assignments. We should investigate or explore the source of our emotions and actions, to be aware is to note feelings such as "I am upset or sad." But to be self-aware is to explore the source of those emotions. If you allow, the Holy Spirit will not only assist and guide you in this endeavor, but he can make it a more efficient process.

Open my eyes, that I may behold wondrous things out of Your law. (Psalm 119:18)

But when the Friend comes, the Spirit of the Truth, he will take you by the hand and guide you into all the truth there is. He won't draw attention to himself, but will make sense out of what is about to happen and, indeed, out of all that I have done and said. (John 16:13, Message Bible)

The Hebrew word for "open" is *galah* and means to uncover, reveal, or strip. Who does the revealing? Who does the uncovering? It is the Holy Spirit who skillfully assists us in this process. But you must be willing. As the Holy Spirit navigates us throughout our journey, he is constantly uncovering hidden motives and agendas. He reveals our weaknesses as well as our strengths, our biases, and our way of thinking. This is necessary if we are to ascend to our greatest heights in him, but we must be willing. Just as obstacles can hinder the GPS from getting us to our destination, so can various obstacles in our lives impact the Holy Spirit's capacity to navigate us to God's intended destination for our lives. You have to spend time with the Holy Spirit through meditation and reflection and worship to accomplish this. Be patient because this will not happen overnight.

I would be remiss if I did not share with you some basic principles that I have found to be foundational throughout my journey. The following foundational principles are not uncommon, and I have found them to be a common thread throughout my studies.

Bible Study

While this may seem to be common knowledge to most believers and while it may appear that most read the Bible on a consistent basis, this is certainly not the case. In general, most Americans continue to view the Bible positively; however, a recent study conducted by the Barna Group (2019) categorized Bible engagement on a continuum as follows:

(1) Bible central: interacts with the Bible frequently such that it is transforming their relationships and shaping their choices

(2) Bible engaged: interacts with the Bible frequently such that it transforms their relationship with God and others

(3) Bible-friendly: interacts with the Bible consistently and that it may be source of spiritual insight and wisdom

(4) Bible neutral: interacts with the Bible sporadically, but it has no spiritual influence

(5) Bible disengaged: interacts with the Bible infrequently, if at all

The results of the study revealed that only 5 percent of individuals are Bible centered, 19 percent are Bible engaged, 19 percent are Bible-friendly, and 57 percent of individuals are Bible disengaged or Bible neutral. The reasons for why people may or may not read the bible vary widely; however, if we want to know God's promises and instructions for life, then we need to read the Bible. Interestingly, a pastry chef needs recipes to prepare desserts, bread, or baked goods until they have mastered their craft; a seamstress uses a pattern to make the perfect dress until he or she has mastered the craft; a conductor uses a score of music to guide the orchestra; and we use a GPS to get to destinations that we are unfamiliar with. The Bible contains the instructions that provide insight to effectively live in this world. Before Joshua began his journey to the Promised Land, God gave him specific instructions.

> This book of the law shall not depart out
> of thy mouth; but thou shalt meditate therein
> day and night, that thou mayest observe to do
> according to all that is written therein: for then

thou shalt make thy way prosperous, and then
thou shalt have good success. (Joshua 1:8)

If Joshua was going to be successful on his journey, then it was imperative that he mused over the Word of God. The Bible contains the instructions you will need to become informed decision-makers throughout your journey.

Thy word is a lamp unto my feet, and a
light unto my path. (Psalm 119:105)

For as the rain cometh down, and the snow
from heaven, and returneth not thither, but
watereth the earth, and maketh it bring forth and
bud, that it may give seed to the sower, and bread
to the eater. So shall my word be that goeth forth
out of my mouth: it shall not return unto me
void, but it shall accomplish that which I please,
and it shall prosper in the thing whereto I sent it.
(Isaiah 55:10, 11)

And we all, with unveiled face, continually
seeing as in a mirror the glory of the Lord, are
progressively being transformed into His image
from [one degree of] glory to [even more] glory,
which comes from the Lord, [who is] the Spirit.
(2 Corinthians 2:18, AMP)

The Word of God reveals to you the character of God. The more you study God's Word and meditate on its teachings, pray, and worship, you take on some of his characteristics. This is a process of evolution and revolution. An evolving of who you were called to be through a revolution of your mind. In her book, *The Prayer Warrior's Way*, Dr. Trimm (2011) discusses the character, Eli, from the movie *The Book of Eli*. She stated that Eli carried the last known Bible on an earth that was decimated by war and that the tyrannical ruler, Carnegie, had searched for this Bible for decades.

> [The Bible's] a weapon. A weapon aimed right at the hearts and minds of the weak and the desperate. It will give us control of them. If we want to rule more than one small…town, we have to have it. People will come from all over, they'll do exactly what I tell 'em if the words are from the book. It's happened before and it'll happen again. All we need is that book. (as cited in Trimm, 2011)

The Bible is indeed a weapon. It has within its pages the capacity to provide the believer with instructions needed for life and godliness. It is up to us to take what is in it and allow the Holy Spirit to navigate us using these very instructions. It is not enough to listen to your favorite televangelist, pastor, or motivational speaker. *You* have got to study the Bible for yourself. Listen, the man who had an infirmity for thirty-eight years had camped out at the Pool of Bethesda waiting for an urban legend to be fulfilled that when an angel came down to "stir" the water, the first person to get in was healed from any infirmity of disease that he or she had. This man had been unsuccessful in his attempts. When Jesus came and saw him in an impotent state, he simply asked him, "Will you be made whole."

The impotent man did not respond with a resounding yes but rather an excuse as to why he was in his current disposition. Ignoring the urban legend, Jesus tells the man to get up off his mat, pick it up, and walk away (John 5:1–8). The man wasn't looking for God to heal him, but he was looking for another man to do it. Don't wait on others to instruct you through biblical concepts; know the Bible for yourself. Study so that you may be empowered to empower others.

> Don't wait for others to empower you or you will be waiting a lifetime. Use the instructions found in the Bible to become empowered! (Donna P. Turner, PHD)

Prayer

Prayer is instrumental to your journey. It is essential, if not imperative, that you have a prayer life if you are going to effectively navigate this journey. Prayer can be defined as a personal communication or petition addressed to a deity, especially in the form of supplication, adoration, praise, contrition, or thanksgiving. St. Augustine of Hippo was considered to be one of the leading early Christian theologians and philosophers whose writings were very influential in the development of Western Christianity and philosophy. His most noted works include *Confessions*, an autobiography of his early life, and *The City of God*, which he wrote to restore the hope of Christians who experienced upheaval at the hands of the Arian Christians. St. Augustine's thoughts on prayer were quite simplistic. He believed that sincere prayer was not found in the multiplicity of words but rather in a sincere desire for God. St. Augustine makes the following statement about prayer:

> Prayer is not the reverberation of sound; it is the articulation of love. It is with the heart rather than the lips that we pray…Therefore, whether we cry to the Lord with the voice of the body— where occasion demands it—or in silence, we must cry from the heart.

Prayer is communication with God. The root word for communication is "commune" which means to converse or talk together with profound intensity or intimacy. It is also described as an interchange of thoughts or feelings. Prayer is about relationship: you communing with God and God communing with you. Prayer is personal. Your relationship with God is personal. How you communicate cannot be dictated by anyone. You are unique, and God relates to you based on your own uniqueness.

I do not pretend to know everything about the Holy Spirit, but our relationship is ongoing similar to any relationship.

> …and he calls his own sheep by name and brings (leads) them out. When he has brought his own sheep outside, he walks on before them, and the sheep follow him because they know his voice. They will never [on any account] follow a stranger, but will run away from him because they do not know the voice of strangers *or* recognize their call. (John 10:3–5, Amplified)

Again, it takes time and patience when getting to know him, but you have to also be patient with yourself. You will learn a lot about yourself as you are getting to know him. You have to learn his ways and how he specifically speaks to you. David did nothing without prayer. With every major move, David enquired of the Lord.

> Then they told David, saying, Behold, the Philistines fight against Keilah, and they rob the threshing floors. Therefore David enquired of the LORD, saying, Shall I go and smite these Philistines? And the LORD said unto David, Go, and smite the Philistines, and save Keilah. (I Samuel 23:1, 2)
>
> And David enquired at the LORD, saying, Shall I pursue after this troop? shall I overtake them? And he answered him, Pursue: for thou shalt surely overtake them, and without fail recover all. (1 Samuel 30:8)
>
> And it came to pass after this, that David enquired of the LORD, saying, Shall I go up into any of the cities of Judah? And the LORD said unto him, Go up. And David said, Whither shall I go up? And he said, Unto Hebron. (2 Samuel 2:1)

Jesus did nothing without praying.

> And in the morning, rising up a great while before day, he went out, and departed into a solitary place, and there prayed. (Mark 1:35)

There are many types of prayers, including the prayer of adoration, confession, thanksgiving, supplication, reception, and obligatory prayer. In a study on Prayer and Subjective Well-Being, Whittington and Scher (2010) used Laird et al.'s (2004) framework to investigate the relationship between the types of prayer and subjective well-being. They describe five types of prayer: (1) prayers of adoration that focus on the worship of God, without any reference to circumstances, needs, or desires; (2) prayers of thanksgiving which are expressions of gratitude toward God, made in reference to specific positive life experiences; (3) prayers of supplication that request specific interventions in life events for oneself or others; (4) prayers of confession which involve the admission of negative behaviors and a request for forgiveness; and (5) prayers of reception which involve waiting on divine wisdom, understanding, or guidance. Whittington and Scher added obligatory prayer to the original framework suggesting that followers are required to pray three and five times a day, respectively. These required prayers consist primarily of fixed prayers repeated at each worship time.

Whittington and Scher found that of the six types of prayers, adoration, thanksgiving, and reception have positive effects on self-esteem, optimism, and meaning of life. Ducharme (2018) suggested that prayer has been shown to be powerful, in at least one way. It triggers the relaxation response, a state of mind-body rest that has been shown to decrease stress, heart rate, and blood pressure, alleviate chronic disease symptoms, and even change gene expression. This state is typically linked to activities like meditation and yoga, and research suggests it can also be found through praying.

Prayer is essential to your journey. Prayer opens up the lines of communication between you and the Holy Spirit. It opens the door for you to share your most intimate secrets, your concerns, your fears, your perceived failures, and your successes. You exchange your burdens, fears, and deepest concerns for his peace while you learn to trust your journey just like *Much Afraid*. Worshipping God for who he is and not what he can do, gratitude for your current disposition, and waiting patiently on his leading are important to your journey!

Worship

A person will *worship* something, have no doubt about that. We may think our tribute is paid in secret in the dark recesses of our hearts, but it will come out. That which dominates our imaginations and our thoughts will determine our lives, and our character. Therefore, it behooves us to be careful what we *worship*, for what we are worshipping we are becoming.

—(Ralph Waldo Emerson)

Prayer and worship, in my estimation, go hand in hand. Prayer cultivates the heart and prepares it for worship, and worship cultivates and deepens your relationship with the Holy Spirit. The most common word used for worship in the New Testament is *proskuneo*, and it means to adore or venerate God. This word occurs sixty times in the New Testament, fifty-seven of which are found in the four gospels, the book of Acts, and the book of Revelation. The term originally carried with it the idea of subjects falling down to kiss the ground before a king or kiss their feet. The literal definition means "to kiss, like a dog licking his master's hand, to fawn or crouch to, to pay homage, reverence, or adore" (Strong).

God loves worship, and he loves worshippers. Worship is heartfelt. It reveals the heart of man. Worship is about priority because whatever and whoever has your heart has your worship (Matthew 6:21). Stone (1998) says that whatever we devote ourselves to, whatever occupies our thoughts, emotions, desires, and decisions and governs the way we live our lives, whether sports, family, work, wealth, fame or pleasure, that, in the broadest sense of the word, is what we worship. The person that has your heart will get your time and attention, and that is the individual that you will follow. You pay homage to that which has you. Worship is a lifestyle and should not be relegated to how long you spend each day in prayer. God loves worship because it reveals the contents of your heart. God loves worship so much so that the scripture records that he actually "seeks" worship or worshippers,

> A time will come, however, indeed it is already here, when the true (genuine) worshipers will worship the Father in spirit and in truth (reality); for the Father is seeking just such people as these as His worshipers. God is a Spirit (a spiritual Being) and those who worship Him must worship *Him* in spirit and in truth (reality). (John 4:23–24, Amplified Bible)
>
> It's who you are and the way you live that count before God. Your worship must engage your spirit in the pursuit of truth. That's the kind of people the Father is out looking for: those who

are simply and honestly *themselves* before him in their worship. God is sheer being itself—Spirit. Those who worship him must do it out of their very being, their spirits, their true selves, in adoration. (John 4:23–24, Message Bible)

There are two important aspects that I would like to highlight from the above passage: God is seeking worshippers, and these worshippers must worship him in spirit and in truth. The first aspect of this passage of scripture indicates that God is actively seeking worshippers. The Greek word for "seeketh" is *zeteo* and means to seek by inquiring, to investigate, to reach a binding (terminal) resolution, and to search by "getting to the bottom of a matter." I was blown away when I first read this definition. The Father investigates and comes to the resolution of those that are true worshippers. He knows those that are truly his, not by their mere confession but rather by the resounding love and adoration of the heart.

The second aspect of this passage of the scripture reveals the character of the worshipper that God seeks—one who must worship him in spirit and in truth. Now, the first part of this verse "in spirit" reveals that worship is a matter of the heart. It is not the external or superficial act of service but rather our true estimation of who he is in our life. Worship is simply intimacy with the one you love. You may be wondering why this is a necessary part of your journey. How can you follow someone that you don't know? How can you trust someone when there is no relationship? When you love and trust someone, you will follow them to the ends of the earth. Again, that doesn't happen overnight. It takes time to get to know someone and to learn their ways, what they like and dislike, what makes them laugh, what makes them cry. Have you ever noticed that the more time you spend with an individual, people begin to say that you and that person mimic each other? It is the same with the Holy Spirit. The more time you spend with him, you learn to trust him and depend on him for everything. This is not easy.

As I mentioned earlier, I like stability, and I do not like surprises. I never liked living my life on the edge but always had some level of respect for those that did. Now I find myself in a place where I have to completely rely on God for everything. It requires a great deal of patience when getting to know God. It requires commitment, obedience, and faith.

Committing to someone means you are dedicating or pledging yourself to that person and all that they represent. When you get married, you promise to love, honor, protect, and obey each other until death do you part. When you take a job, you're making a commitment to show up and do the job well, and your employer makes a commitment to pay you. There are smaller commitments as well. If you said you'd meet a friend at six, that's a commitment; show up on time, or your friend will be mad. You can speak of commitment as a quality. Staying after school for a study group shows your commitment to good grades. When you commit to God, you are pledging in essence your life, your talent, your time, and your purpose to him. Obedience may be described as a form of social influence whereby a person yields to explicit instructions or orders from an authority figure. When you love someone, obedience is not a problem (not that we don't have occasional mishaps). When you truly love someone, you try your best not to hurt them by honoring their requests.

> For the [true] love of God is this: that we
> do His commands [keep His ordinances and
> are mindful of His precepts and teaching]. And
> these orders of His are not irksome (burdensome,
> oppressive, or grievous). (1 John 5:3, Amplified)

Faith is the trust or confidence in and loyalty to a person or deity. The Greek word for "faith," *pistis,* is described as a gift from God and is *never* something that can be produced by people. In other words, faith for the believer is God's *divine persuasion* and therefore distinct from human belief or confidence yet involving it. The Lord continuously births faith in the yielded believer so they can know what he prefers, i.e., the persuasion of his will (retrieved from http://biblehub.com/greek/4102.htm). Commitment, obedience, and faith are progressive.

> Your heart of devotion and obedience is not
> in vain. Who knows but God how many people
> have come near to you and were forever changed
> simply by the fragrance of his love in you? Who
> knows but God if he will put you before kings
> and leaders to speak the truth, redirecting the
> future of nations? Who knows when that small
> crack in the dam of our enemy's plans will give
> way and God's glory will truly cover the earth as
> the sea? Do not become distracted or discouraged
> by the death around you. Death must always give
> way when the life of Christ enters the picture.
> (Amy Layne Litzelman, 2010)

Again, it takes time to cultivate commitment, obedience, and faith. Commitment and obedience are birthed out of adoration and love for someone. The more you love God, the less resistant you are to his will for your life. Worship will bring you to a place of love and adoration. Worship helped me to focus on God rather than on myself and my circumstances. Worship and the Word of God enabled me to know him in ways that I never thought I could, and I am still learning. I dare not take one step without him.

Prayer, worship, and Bible study are the foundations to the life of every believer. The last two principles that I believe are essential to your journey are Napolean Hill's *definite purpose* and *accurate thought*.

Definite Purpose

In his book, *the Law of Success*, Napoleon Hill (1925) discusses the importance of having a definite purpose, that specific thing that you were created to do. Over the course of fourteen years, Hill claimed to have interviewed or analyzed fifteen thousand people. From his analyses, Hill found that 95 percent of the people interviewed were failures and only 5 percent were deemed successful. Hill defined failure as one who had failed to find happiness and the ordinary necessities of life without struggle. Hill also found that the 95 percent who were classified as failures were in that class because they had no definite purpose in life, while the successful 5 percent not only had purpose that was definite but also had a definite plan for the attainment of their purposes. More than seventy-five years later, not much has changed regarding people's disposition relative to purpose.

A study conducted by the Barna Group in 2013 found that three-quarters of US adults (75 percent) say they are looking for ways to live a more meaningful life. Whether such meaning is found in family, career, church, side projects, or elsewhere, these are all questions of vocation, the way in which people feel "called" to certain types of work and life choices. This study also revealed that among Christians, there is an additional question: "What does God want me to do with my life?" According to this study, only 40 percent of practicing Christians say they have a clear sense of God's calling on their lives. Of the 75 percent that say they are looking for ways to live more meaningful lives, 56 percent state that they want to make a difference in the world; 46 percent are afraid of making the wrong career choice; 25 percent state that they have clear goals as to where they want to be in five years; and only 20 percent have an idea of what God wants them to do with their lives. This study comprised four separate nationwide studies conducted between May and August 2013 using telephone and online interviews among 4,495 adults. Several studies have found purpose to be a predictor of longevity and well-being. Hill and Turiano (2014) found that purpose was a good predictor of longevity across adulthood. In an earlier study, Boyle et al. (2009) found that having a greater purpose in life is associated with health and well-being in old age. In his book entitled, *Kingdom Principles: Preparing for Kingdom Experience and Expansion*, Dr. Myles Munroe (2006) makes the following statement about purpose:

> The greatest tragedy in life is not death but life without a purpose—life with the wrong priorities. Life's greatest challenge is in knowing what to do…The greatest mistake in life is to be busy but not effective. Life's greatest failure is to be successful in the wrong assignment.

It is never too late to find out your purpose in life. Your passions, your strengths, and your life experiences inform your purpose. When you discover your purpose, you can be more targeted and selective in your activities. Ask the Holy Spirit to show you. Oftentimes, our purpose is something that we do without thinking. It's just that you have to carve out time to figure it out. Please don't limit yourself. Your purpose is vast, and for some of you, it will be intimidating. If you have children, help them to discover their purpose early in life. Expose them to activities that will assist them in determining their likes and dislikes. They don't have to wander somewhat aimlessly in life like some of us did waiting on the validation of others. Empower them *Now*!

When I first read his book, it revolutionized my thinking. I had what I believed to be a good foundation built on prayer, worship, and study; however, I lacked a *definite purpose*. Not only was I unsure about my purpose, I was so busy coveting everyone else's purpose that it was difficult to distinguish my purpose in life.

> When you fail to discover your purpose,
> you will find yourself living in the shadows of
> others. (Donna P. Turner, PhD)

I prayed about my purpose and just could not figure out what I was specifically created to do. I surmised that since I had taught for so long, then, surely, this was my definite purpose in life. I enjoyed teaching but not in confined settings. I continued to pray, and one day it hit me—part of my purpose was what I had been doing all along. I did this one particular thing every day, albeit in various contexts. I was a writer. It took me some time to become comfortable with this. I had been told by some of my former teachers and tutors that I was not a good writer, which fueled my insecurity and made me question my ability to write. I am sure they meant well, but when you are already struggling with insecurity, the slightest bit of criticism can be detrimental. Thus, I had little confidence in my writing ability, so it was practically inconceivable for me to consider myself a writer.

The Holy Spirit knew this about me and therefore knew what settings to place me in that would build my confidence in my writing ability. My pastor gave me the opportunity to write an article for him based on one of his teachings, and my doctoral program helped build my confidence in my ability. These endeavors forced me to write even when I did not want to. Interestingly, prior to writing articles at church and the abundance of writing I did during my doctorate, I had been journaling for about six or seven years. Every day or every other day, I would write in my journal about everything that was going in my life. This was a part of my morning meditation. I would always start my journal with *Good Morning, Holy Spirit,* and I would begin telling him about everything that was going on in my life. Interestingly, from my writings, I also found that my relationship with the Holy Spirit had changed—instead of starting off my journal with *Good Morning, Holy Spirit,* I found myself writing, *Good Morning, My Love.* I did not realize this until I was looking over some of my journal excerpts from years back. So I had been writing quite some time before I realized that this was my definite purpose. It would be a couple of years before I would make peace with my overarching purpose.

Napoleon Hill makes the following comments regarding *definite purpose*:

1. A *definite purpose* that is deliberately fixed in the mind and held there, with the determination to realize it, finally saturates the entire subconscious mind until it automatically influences the physical action of the body toward the attainment of that purpose.

2. Your *definite purpose* in life should be selected with deliberate care, and after it has been selected, it should be written out and placed where you will see it at least once a day.

3. The subconscious mind may be likened to a magnet, and when it has been vitalized and thoroughly saturated with any *definite purpose*, it has a decided tendency to attract all that is necessary for the fulfillment of that purpose.

4. All great leaders base their leadership upon a *definite purpose*. Followers are willing to follow when they know that their leader is a person with a definite purpose who has the courage to back up that purpose with action.

5. Until a man selects his *definite purpose* in life, he dissipates his energies and spreads his thoughts over so many subjects and in so many different directions that they lead not to power but to indecision and weakness.

Finally, Hill writes, "Suppose your definite purpose is far above your present station in life. What of it? It is your privilege—nay, your DUTY, to aim high in life. You owe it to yourself and to the community in which you live to set a high standard for yourself."

In her book, *The Forty Day Soul Fast*, Dr. Trimm (2011) stated that some of the most prevalent and misunderstood things that keep people from running with purpose and certainty are the toxic thoughts and lethal strongholds within the soul; memories of painful experiences, destructive habits, emotional attachments, misplaced desires, limiting beliefs, and narrow objectives undermine purpose, meaning, and lasting fulfillment. She further suggests that if these thoughts are unaddressed and left to perpetuate in the soul of the believer, then it is these very thoughts that can render the believer incapacitated to fulfill that which they were born to do. You must work to cultivate a thoughtful life that is conducive to the perpetuity of imagination and genius. This is not easy. It takes time, energy, and practice.

Accurate Thought

Lastly, I have found one principle to be essential and common to those who have lived a purposeful life. This principle, properly called *accurate thought*, permeates every aspect of our life. Hill thought that accurate thought involves two fundamental rules that all who indulge in must observe. He suggested that accurate thought required the "thinking" individual to be able to separate facts from mere information. He states:

> That you may understand the importance
> of distinguishing between facts and mere infor-
> mation, study that type of man who is guided
> entirely by what he hears, the type who is influ-
> enced by all the whisperings of the all the winds

of gossip, who accepts, without analysis, all that he reads in the newspapers and judges others by what their enemies and competitors and contemporaries say about them. [p. 269]

He suggests:

> The accurate thinker knows that the newspapers are not always accurate in their reports, and he also knows that what they say usually carries more falsehood than truth. [p.270]

Hill conceptualized accurate thought as the separation of facts from information. In other words, Hill thought it necessary that the accurate thinker be able to separate propaganda or that which is false or exaggerated from the truth because he knew the impact that propaganda could have on the psyche. Perception informs accurate thought. Remember, the children of Israel never thought they could inhabit the Promised Land, and so they did not. Thoughts are powerful and, through the guidance of the Holy Spirit, can cultivate positive thinking.

> Summing it all up, friends, I'd say you'll do best by filling your minds and meditating on things true, noble, reputable, authentic, compelling, gracious—the best, not the worst; the beautiful, not the ugly; things to praise, not things to curse. (Philippians 4:8, Message)

Imagine training your mind by strategically focusing your thoughts on God's purpose for your life. Imagine cultivating your thought life by creating an environment free of distractions and negativity by simply training your mind to focus on purpose and all that it entails.

The efficaciousness of your thought life greatly depends on you. You have seen glimpses of inventions that could make you a millionaire, yet it is difficult or even impossible for those heaven-born ideas to become realized because there is too much natural and/or spiritual refuse in your atmosphere. This refuse can hinder you from getting the clarity you need regarding these heaven-born creations; it can hinder communication between you and the Holy Spirit preventing you from getting the directions you will need in order to proceed to the next destination in your life. This refuse can include gossip, too much radio/television, busyness, and jealousy and strife to name a few. Again, the efficaciousness of your thought life greatly depends on you. Your thoughts can catapult you to your greatest heights with the aid of the Holy Spirit, or they can enslave you to the catacombs of your shallow expectations or the shallow opinions rendering you incapacitated to purpose, thereby hindering your journey to your set Promised Land.

Every idea begins with a thought. It would be ten years before George de Mestral's conception of Velcro would become realized in 1951, and four years later before he would receive a patent for what was once a simple idea in his mind. Walter Hunt had no idea that his inventions, the safety pin and sewing machine, would be widely used today. He sold the patent for the safety pin for $400 to pay a $15 debt.

Orville and Wilbur Wright were credited with inventing and building the world's first successful airplane and making the first controlled, powered, and sustained heavier-than-air human flight on December 17, 1903. Thomas Alva Edison had a tremendous influence on modern life, contributing inventions such as the light bulb, the phonograph, and the motion picture camera, as well as improving the telegraph and telephone. Edison was self-taught. Around the age of twelve, he established a small newspaper called the *Grand Trunk Herald.* Alexander Graham Bell was awarded the first US patent for the telephone in 1876. Dr. Charles Drew was an African-American surgeon who pioneered methods of storing blood plasma for transfusion and organized the first large-scale blood bank in the United States. Jan Matzeliger developed the "shoe lacing machine" which increased the percentage of shoes made daily by roughly 900 percent. The list goes on and on. All of these ideas began with a thought years before these ideas became realized. If you are going to change your world, your sphere of influence, then you must have accurate thought. Dr. Myles Munroe (2008) stated that ideas are vital, but our way of thinking about ideas is even more significant. When we receive ideas, our brains begin to work on analyzing them to see whether we accept them or not. If we accept the idea, our conscious minds take them and transfer them to an account called the subconscious mind that stores them in our long-term memory. Consider the following posited by Munroe:

✓ The accumulation of the ideas we accept becomes our belief system, our philosophy of life. These are the ideas that we embrace, retain, and live by. All of us are philosophers whether we realize it or not.

✓ You live the ideas you accept. You become your thoughts. People can make you who they want you to be, if you accept their words into your life.

✓ The average human being never discovers who he or she is. They become what everyone expects.

Everything begins with a thought. Thoughts are potent. This is why you must be careful of the thoughts that you allow to linger in your consciousness (Munroe, 2008). Mahatma Gandhi said, "Man is but the product of his thoughts, what he thinks, he becomes." In other words, whatever you believe you will become, you will. Your ability to grow is only limited by your imagination in this world.

I used to think that I could not go on
And life was nothing but an awful song
But now I know the meaning of true love
I'm leaning on the everlasting arms

If I can see it, then I can do it
If I just believe it, there's nothing to it
Chorus
I believe I can fly
I believe I can touch the sky
I think about it every night and day
Spread my wings and fly away
I believe I can soar
I see me running through that open door
I believe I can fly
I believe I can fly

I believe I can fly

(Robert S. Kelly, 1996)

I am sure that there are many interpretations of this song; however, I would like to frame my interpretation within the context for this book. Note the fourth line of the first stanza, "I'm leaning on the everlasting arms." When you lean on the Holy Spirit for inspiration and guidance for every part of your journey, he will provide the road-map and guideposts you will need to get to your next station in life. The third line of the chorus, "I think about it every night and day, spread my wings and fly away," suggests that when continual thought is given to a particular thing, it is only a matter of time before it becomes realized. Your thoughts have the capacity to change your present stance in this life. Your thoughts have the capacity to catapult you from mundane to the magnificent. What will you do with your thoughts?

> If your thoughts are inferior, your life will be inferior; but if your thoughts are lofty and honorable, you are laying the foundation to live accordingly...If your life is going to change, you must think for a change. You are always only one thought away from changing your life. (Dr. Cindy Trimm, *Commanding Your Morning*)

Pearls of Wisdom #9. Prayer opens up the lines of communication between you and the Holy Spirit. Prayer cultivates the heart and prepares it for worship, and worship cultivates and deepens your relationship with the Holy Spirit.

Pearls of Wisdom #10. Know your purpose! If you fail to know your purpose, then you will forever live in the shadows of expectation of others!

Chapter 5

THE JOURNEY OF A LIFETIME!

*Don't be discouraged if the people around
you don't see what you see in your dream.
Most great people were doubted in the
beginning of their journey to greatness.*
—Edmond Mbiaka

I began writing this book a few years ago, and as I have mentioned, I have experienced many ups and downs. The person I currently am is different than the person who started writing this book a few years back. She is confident and sure of herself. Every disappointment has made me stronger. The hurt, shame, and guilt that once shackled me to my past have now catapulted me into my future. My mess has become my *muse*. I am a masterpiece in the making.

Several years ago, I was given a book that was simple but needed during that time period of my life. She strategically placed crosses on different pages of the book to indicate that in the most difficult times of my life, the Holy Spirit would be right there leading me every step of the way. This book, *Oh the Places You'll Go,* by far is one of my most favorite books of all times. Remember, you have been called to greatness. Your journey to greatness will be gratifying and difficult. You will have moments when you will simply want to quit. In agony, Jesus asked the Father as he agonized over his impending assignment, if there was any way possible that he could abnegate his mission.

> Going a little ahead, he fell on his face, pray-
> ing, "My Father, if there is any way, get me out of
> this. But please, not what I want. You, what do
> *you* want?" (Matthew 26:39, Message Bible)

Despite the anguish, pain, and persecution, Jesus gave up his life and all he knew so that we could live. He completed his journey, thereby fulfilling his destiny and thereby given the name above all names. He was crowned the King of kings.

During some of the most difficult times of my life, I have told God that I no longer want this assignment because the trial was too much for me to bear. It was during those times that I learned to worship and trust God. Many of us have dreams that we believe God has placed in our hearts; however, we allow our wilderness experiences to thwart the dreams or plans that God has given us. I was in the wilderness when I started writing this book. Now, I am entering my Promised Land. But know that it is in your wilderness that you will experience your greatest successes, your greatest triumphs, and your greatest breakthroughs.

> It is in the quiet crucible of your personal
> private sufferings that your noblest dreams are
> born and Gods greatest gifts are given in com-

pensation for what you have been through. (Wintley Phipps)

As I conclude this book, I leave you with the familiar words of select excerpts from *Oh the Places You'll Go* that is dear to my heart. Every time you find yourself in unfamiliar territory, remember that your GPS is right there to get you back on track.

Congratulations! Today is your day. You're off to Great Places! You're off and away!

You have brains in your head. You have feet in your shoes. You can steer yourself any direction you choose. You're on your own.

And you know what you know. And YOU are the guy who'll decide where to go. You'll look up and down streets. Look 'em over with care. About some you will say, "I don't choose to go there."

With your head full of brains and your shoes full of feet, you're too smart to go down any not-so-good street. And you may not find any you'll want to go down. In that case, of course, you'll head straight out of town.

Out there things can happen and frequently do to people as brainy and footsy as you. And when things start to happen, don't worry. Don't stew. Just go right along. You'll start happening too…All Alone! Whether you like it or not, Alone will be something you'll be quite a lot. And when you're alone, there's a very good chance you'll meet things that scare you right out of your pants. There are some, down the road between hither and yon, that can scare you so much you won't want to go on. But on you will go through the weather be foul. On you will go though your enemies prowl. On you will go though the Hakken-Kraks howl.

Onward up many a frightening creek, though your arms may get sore and your sneakers may leak. On and on you will hike. And I know you'll hike far, and face up to your problems whatever they are. You'll get mixed up, of course, as you already know. You'll get mixed up with many strange birds as you go. So be sure when you step, Step with care and great tact and remember that Life's a Great Balancing Act. Just never forget to be dexterous and deft. And never mix up your right foot with your left. And Will You Succeed? YES! You Will Indeed! (Dr. Seuss, 1990)

References

Boyle, P. A., Barnes, L. L., Buchman, A. S., & Bennett, D. A. (2009). Purpose in life is associated with mortality among community-dwelling older persons. Psychosomatic Medicine, 71(5), 574-579. doi:10.1097/psy.0b013e3181a5a7c0

Chopra, D., & Tanzi, R. E. (2013). Super brain. Bath: Paragon.

Douglass, F. (1962). *Life and times of Frederick Douglass.* New York, New York: Macmillan.

Ducharme, J. (2018, February 15). The Connection Between Religion, Praying and Living Longer. Retrieved from http://time.com/5159848/do-religious-people-live-longer.

Halley, H. H. (2007). Halleys Bible handbook with the New International Version. Grand Rapids, MI: Zondervan.

Hill, P. L., & Turiano, N. A. (2014). Purpose in Life as a Predictor of Mortality Across Adulthood. Psychological Science, 25(7), 1482-1486.

Hill, N. (2010). *The law of success: Original 1925 edition.* Beverly, MA: Orne Publishing.

Hurnard, H. (1993). Hinds feet on high places. Wheaton, Ill: Tyndale House.

Laird, S. P., Snyder, C. R., Rapoff, M. A., & Green, S. (2004). Measuring private prayer: Development, validation, and clinical application of the multidimensional prayer inventory. The International Journal for the Psychology of Religion, 14, 251–272.

Optical illusions show how we see: Beau Lotto. (2009, October 08). Retrieved from https://youtu.be/mf5otGNbkuc

Maraboli, S. (2013). Unapologetically you: Reflections on life and the human experience. Port Washington, NY: A Better Today.

Munroe, M. (2006). Kingdom principles: Preparing for kingdom experience and expansion. Shippensburg, PA: Destiny Image.

Munroe, M. (2008). *In charge: Finding the leader within you.* London: Faith Words.

Packer, J. I. (2013). Knowing God. London: Hodder & Stoughton.

Trimm, C. (2011). The 40-day soul fast: Your journey to authentic living. Shippensburg, PA: Destiny Image.

Whittington, Bramdon L. and Scher, Steven J., "Prayer and subjective well-being: An examination of six different types of prayer" (2010). Faculty Research and Creative Activity. 31. http://thekeep.eiu.edu/psych_fac/31

ABOUT THE AUTHOR

A labama native, Donna P. Turner is passionate about educating and empowering people to live an authentic and purposeful life. Always concerned about other's perceptions of her, she lived most of her life trying to please people as she looked for validation of self. Against all odds, Donna quit her job of fourteen years and never looked back and went on to complete her PhD at The University of Alabama in 2011. She has over twenty years of experience in public and higher education, education administration, and educational research. Donna has become a successful educator, noted speaker, and author. She is the founder of The Donna P. McCullum Foundation for Educational Excellence, a nonprofit organization that provides scholarships to minority girls entering their first year of college.

CPSIA information can be obtained
at www.ICGtesting.com
Printed in the USA
BVHW080829030521
606328BV00004B/99